14.00

DATE DUE			

—*Webb S. Fiser* is an Associate Professor of Political Science in the Maxwell Graduate School of Citizenship and Public Affairs at Syracuse University where he organized and conducted the first Integration Seminar in the Metropolitan Studies Program. From 1958-59, Professor Fiser was Principal Planner in the Office of Urban Renewal for the city of Syracuse and is currently a member of the Citizen's Council on Urban Renewal, the advisory body to the Mayor of Syracuse.

MASTERY OF THE METROPOLIS

W E B B   S .   F I S E R

MASTERY OF THE METROPOLIS

GREENWOOD PRESS, PUBLISHERS
WESTPORT, CONNECTICUT

Library of Congress Cataloging in Publication Data

Fiser, Webb S
    Mastery of the metropolis.

    Reprint of the ed. published by Prentice-Hall,
Englewood Cliffs, N. J., in series: A Spectrum
book.
    Includes bibliographical references.
    1. Metropolitan areas--United States.   T.   Title.
[HT334.U5F5 1980]   306.7'6   80-23244
ISBN 0-313-22732-2 (lib. bdg.)

Reprinted with the permission of Prentice-Hall Inc.

Reprinted in 1981 by Greenwood Press
A division of Congressional Information Service, Inc.
88 Post Road West, Westport, Connecticut 06881

Printed in the United States of America

10 9 8 7 6 5 4 3 2 1

Preface

This book is an attempt to provide perspective on our metropolitan problems. It is based upon an old interest in our urban problems which was stimulated by Walter Blucher in 1946-7 while the author was a graduate student at the University of Chicago. More recently this work derives from the author's search at the Maxwell School for a better way of teaching students and training professionals in the complexities of our urban world. It also arises out of the author's experience as the principal planner for urban renewal in the City of Syracuse.

While the work is based upon the experience of the author, it is not based upon original academic research. It is rather an attempt to reflect upon the large body of research now being done by others, to explore the range of values involved in approaching our urban problems, to find significant concepts for approaching these problems and to look at the strategy of change.

No attempt is made to provide a complete guide to materials in the field. References have been chosen according to those works which the author found most useful, those which he believes the general reader can use to best advantage and those which have been quoted or commented upon. Few of the individual ideas are original with the author, although in many instances it is now impossible to say what their origin was. The author hopes that the attempt to put the ideas together in an overview of this complex subject will prove useful.

The author's intellectual debts extend to so many colleagues and practitioners across the United States that an attempt at enumeration is fruitless. However, I must mention my colleagues at the Maxwell School who have been constant sources of stimulation—Professors Max Bloom, Warner Bloomberg, Jr., Guthrie Birkhead, Jesse Burkhead, Roscoe Martin, Paul Meadows, Frank Munger and Dean

Harlan Cleveland. Special mention should be made of Professor Spencer D. Parratt with whom I have shared an office these past five years. We have discussed urban problems almost daily during this time and my debt to him is greater than I can recount.

Of course, any errors, blind spots, or other inadequacies are entirely the responsibility of the author.

Table of Contents

1   Introduction: Problems and Purposes   1

2   The Future of the Metropolis 11

     Housing 11

     The Neighborhood 21

     Downtown 27

     Other Goals 35

3   The Context of National Forces 37

     Technology 37

     Economic Forces 42

     Political Values 48

     Social Forces 53

4   The Intermingling of Public and Private . . 61

     Development of Governmental
       Regulation 62

     The New Private Role—Metro-
       politan Development 66

     The New Private Role—The
       Central City 73

     The Case of Zoning 78

     Public Education 81

5   The Case of Urban Renewal 88

     A Workable Program 89

     An Urban Renewal Project 98

ix

The Metropolitan Context 103
Summary 106

6 Governmental Reorganization 108
The Federal Government 109
The State 112
The Lesson of Toronto 117
The Metropolitan Community 121
Dade County 125
Inter-County Supervisors Com-
mittee 128

7 Citizen Action 131
Neighborhood Rehabilitation 132
Citywide Organizations 134
Central Business District 136
The Metropolitan Approach 137
A Model 141

8 Mastery of the Metropolis 151
Perspectives 151
The Range of Discretion 155
Political Values 160
Strategy of Progress 164
Epilogue 168

MASTERY OF THE METROPOLIS

1

Introduction: Problems and Purposes

In recent years we have become aware of something fundamentally wrong with our new urban areas. Several scholars and planners saw the signs in the Thirties or earlier, H. G. Wells saw them at the turn of the century.[1]

> You will find that many people who once slept and worked and reared their children and worshipped and bought all in one area, are now, as it were, *delocalized;* they have overflowed their containing locality, and they live in one area, they work in another, and they go to shop in a third. And the only way in which you can localize them again is to expand your areas to their new scale.

Since 1945 our prosperity, increased birth rate, and advancing technology have greatly accelerated the process of urban growth. Our urban expansion has resulted in a sprawling metropolitan region made possible by the private automobile, the extension of power and telephone connections, all-weather roads, the lowly septic tank, and other technological changes. The symptoms of discomfort are now known to all of us: the traffic congestion of our central cities caused by increased dependence on the private automobile for movement; the rapid decline in our systems of mass transit; the shortage of downtown parking space; the strain on the water supply; the great expense of providing sewage disposal in a diffused

[1] H. G. Wells, "A Paper on Administrative Areas Read Before the Fabian Society," Appendix to *Mankind in the Making* (New York: Charles Scribner's Sons, 1904), p. 379.

pattern of suburban and urban-rural fringe development; the spectacle of a wealthy society permitting suburban development without adequate parks or recreational space; the appropriation of prime agricultural land for suburban expansion and the consequent elimination of desirable open space; the enormous increase in school costs in some of our districts and the threatening revolt of even fairly wealthy suburbs against these costs; the need for increasing our hospital resources on a rational basis; the deterioration of large industrial, commercial, and residential areas of our central cities; the decline of our central business districts; the migration of minority groups into our cities and the general increase of socio-economic segregation in residential areas. These are a few of the irritations we have come to refer to as the problems of our metropolitan areas.[2]

The forces which have created the metropolitan explosion will not abate in the near future. If our growth continues, the population of our metropolitan areas may increase by as much as 40,-000,000 people in the next 15 years.[3] Within the next 40 years our urban population will probably be double or more. We will not be able to assess our situation at our leisure and decide what to do. For the indefinite future our difficulties are piling up at an accelerating rate, just like the rate of change in our technology. The technical and organizational inventions which are transforming our urban existence will create problems at an even more rapid rate in the future than in the past. We face a crisis of political and social organization.

Although the problem of metropolitan regions today is, national, indeed international, in scope, we have hesitated to raise the whole question in one forum. We attack only the aspect of water, or of sewage, or of the city slum. We improvise partial solutions to the most pressing difficulties. The federal government adopts a new highway program, the state a new health and hospital plan, and the local community designs a new civic or cultural center, but no

[2] Many of these problems have been well chronicled by the Editors of Fortune in The Exploding Metropolis (Garden City, New York: Doubleday & Company, Inc., 1958).
[3] For population projections see Phillip Hauser, "The Challenge of Metropolitan Growth," Urban Land, December, 1958.

one is responsible for making sure that all the federal programs which impinge on the metropolitan region make parts of a coherent whole. Nor is anyone responsible for making sure that all the state programs fit into a general scheme. Within the metropolitan region itself, no authority exists which has the power to harmonize local plans. And certainly there is no instrument for guaranteeing that the federal, state, and local planners will work within a single rational framework.

There is a lesson to be learned from the Founding Fathers who met in Philadelphia in 1787. The problems under the Articles of Confederation had become so many and fundamental that there was no way out except a thorough reappraisal of the whole matter of government. They had the national quandary of a central government without financial resources, without power to deal with foreign commerce or end practices destructive to inter-state commerce, unable to protect the frontier from Indian raids, too weak to provide the financial and legal stability which alone could make progress possible. We too are now confronted with problems demanding far greater governmental authority than is now available for coping with them. Today we are confronted with mushrooming metropolitan regions tied inchoately together by bonds of work, trade, business, markets, leisure, culture, and philanthropy. In similar circumstances our forefathers made the bold decision to create a governmental authority commensurate with the new problems. They knew the virtues of local rule, but they also knew the danger of attempting to meet great new difficulties with means hopelessly inadequate. They knew that their political arrangements were obsolete; that their dream of liberty, equality, and material progress depends upon fashioning a governmental system to make it possible. They knew the danger of perpetuating a political system which attaches men to sectional or state interests and leaves no one to speak for the common interest. Especially they knew that political competition is good, but that competition without a forum for resolving the issues leads to paralysis.

We are confronted with a similar situation, but have not yet had the wisdom to approach it in a systematic way. We have hardly dared to consider the possibility of raising the enormous complex of problems in our metropolitan region and simply asking what is the rational way out. It is time that we raised the basic question of how we can get an institutional framework which will make it possible to treat the metropolitan region as a coherent whole. This means that we must have new groupings of governmental authority. We must invent machinery of government with sufficient power to resolve the inevitable conflicts. We can no longer tolerate myriad independent power sources, each with the capacity to thwart the rational development of the whole. Conflicting opinions about the future of the metropolitan area are desirable; but conflict without a referee is like a street brawl in which everyone loses.

Those who are trying to plan the metropolitan region have a sense of frustration, of gaining results far less satisfactory than the potentialities warrant. Our creativity, our imagination, our hopes for a better way of living, are lost in the void to which we must address them. And soon we cease to dream; we accept the dirt, congestion, loss of time, cramped quarters, and lack of open space, as primitive man accepted Fate. We devote all our energies to ameliorating those conditions that approach the intolerable.

We can train more people to deal somewhat more effectively with the problems of the metropolitan region, but in the present situation we must train them as repairmen, experts at keeping an obsolete machine from stopping altogether. But if we want our future to depend upon social architects and engineers rather than upon repairmen we must provide a system that has a place for them.

Not many years ago most of industry placed little emphasis upon research. The scientists who are now doing the planning and dreaming for American industry only recently began to do so on a large scale when an institution was created which called forth their talents—the modern corporation with its research and development arm. We will get the similar kind of planning and dreaming the metropolitan area needs when we create a system which has the capacity to take plans and dreams seriously. As long as magnificent ideas must be addressed to everyone in general and no one in particular, we will get few of them.

There is no single solution for all cities. To advocate an ideal solution for all metropolitan areas would be to commit the error of those South American countries which adopted the American constitution without adaptation. Since there is no single organizational pattern to act as panacea, our purpose is to put the problem in its broadest perspective and to suggest a general approach through which each city may find the answer appropriate to its individuality.

Our difficulties derive from more than the fragmentation of governmental units. The creation of adequate political authority would be an enormous aid to progress, but it does not guarantee it. Creating a more desirable urban environment depends upon a combination of private and governmental action. Building and housing codes, zoning ordinances, prosecution of nuisances, planning of highways and community facilities—all these can help provide a minimum standard of social amenities but they cannot create an environment which is a delight to experience and a beauty to behold. The greater part of the character of our cities is the result of private action. Government can be a help or a hindrance but it cannot do the whole job itself.

The quality of our cities depends upon the architectural taste of merchants and bankers, the imagination of realtors and builders, the sensitivity of architects and engineers, the thoughtfulness of industrialists, the resources and good taste of educational institutions, the richness of religious expression, the pride of homeowners, the habits of renters, the depth and breadth of our cultural strivings, and countless other private manifestations of our values and desires.

In the private sphere we encounter a difficulty analagous to the political fragmentation. The citizen is seldom involved as *citizen* but rather as a member of an economic or other such group. Most private interest in the city is expressed through organizations concerned with but a fraction of the city's life. The voices we hear are the Chamber of Commerce, the AFL-CIO, the Manufacturer's Association, the Real Estate Board, or various social or cultural organizations. Seldom do these organizations ask the citizen to think about the total city, to dream about the full potentialities of his urban existence. Rather the focus is upon the need for parking, new highways, an adjustment of assessments, the re-zoning of an area, the need to encourage new industry, the coming water shortage, the need for an industrial or fine arts museum, or any other special issue which is dear to the hearts of some group. Too often the consequence of lack of cultural planning has been that all these activities are undernourished.

Our cultural planning should be related to our educational planning; so far they seldom meet. The locating of new industry is related to the planning of recreation and residential areas but they do not often find their way into the same area of discussion. This age of specialization has the unfortunate concomitant that no one is responsible for the whole. Few even think about it.

Nevertheless, we have made some progress. Most communities have a Council of Social Agencies which provides some planning of the total private social welfare needs of the community. In a few communities a Council of Cultural Agencies has been established. These make possible financial contributions to the cultural development of the community. The individual is freed from the hopeless task of deciding which needs are most urgent. A council can determine priorities and concentrate its funds for maximum advantage. In this field as in others we are coming to the conclusion that an imperfect plan is probably better than none. However, we are still talking about a partial plan.

In the field of private actions few ways exist for the individual or group to discuss—let alone decide—whether a good private decision is also a decision for the common good. The structure of our private associations leads us to deal with the particular matter in relative isolation from other concerns, and from citizenship as a whole.

We need a way to bring the various private and public perspectives to bear upon decision-making.

Nowhere is this more evident than in the revitalization of "downtown." Public action alone cannot do it. A few private individuals usually do not possess sufficient power to do it. The process requires bringing a complex of private interests and activities into harmony with a complex of governmental actions. Effective land-use planning in the metropolitan area is even more complicated because of the welter of governmental jurisdictions involved and often because of less than common cause among the private parties.

This specialized and fragmented structure tends to determine the character of public discussion. As one listens to the debate a feeling of unreality often develops. The question of whether a particular area should create a sewer district may be debated with great heat, when the real question is how much broader an area could deal with cluster of water supply, sanitary sewage, and run-off problems. In some instances the issue will even branch out into questions of stream pollution, water recreation and land-use control, but since the structure of our institutions has only raised the question of a sewer district, the debate occurs on that issue. A centralized school district may ask itself what to do about its exceptional children when the proper context can only be provided on a broader base because there are so few exceptional children in the given district. A central city may ask how it can provide more middle-income housing or public housing, but the only suitable open land is outside the city. A neighborhood may want to rehabilitate itself, but success depends upon the cooperation of local government, lending institutions, and perhaps a branch plant of a national corporation.

It is characteristic of most important issues in the metropolitan area that they cannot be sensibly approached within the confines of the jurisdiction or organization where they are now raised. The quality of public discussion will improve when we provide an organizational structure within which the broader questions can be raised and particular issues can be referred to their total context. The lack of an institutional framework for carrying on the discussion frustrates the hope of action.

There has been little public interest because the structure within which people have been working cannot arouse it. Newspapers now often raise general questions but they are addressed to so broad an audience as seldom to provide a challenge. Is it any wonder that we are subject to apathy when the system raises the wrong issues? Is it any wonder that few talk boldly about the future when our institutions cannot consider truly imaginative proposals? The need for more effective organization is primarily a need to free the mind, to permit the raising of fundamental issues, to get an audience with capacity to act upon the dreams men are capable of dreaming. Only when we understand the potential will we insist upon the reorganization of our means.

Progress in reshaping our urban environment cannot proceed much faster than public understanding and consent. Therefore, urban redevelopment and metropolitan planning can be seen as the consequence of an educated public. The signs of increasing public concern are all about us. The agendas of the Leagues of Women Voters, Chambers of Commerce, Manufacturers' Associations, and labor unions indicate the great growth in interest in urban problems. Many new organizations have been created recently to deal with specific ones; even in some cases with the total complex. Approximately 900 urban renewal projects are in the stage of survey and planning or of execution. The shift in interest toward the need for approaching our urban problems on a comprehensive basis is indicated by the new perspective adopted by ACTION (The American Council to Improve our Neighborhoods). As their work progressed it became clear that neighborhood revitalization could occur satisfactorily only in the context of a comprehensive plan for the development of the whole urban area.

Most of this rapid increase in public interest and understanding was spurred by problems which directly affected the convenience, profits, or tax rate of individuals and businesses. The cost of slums, juvenile delinquency, residential development blocked by sewage or water problems, traffic jams and overcrowded schools drove home the lesson that something had to be done. Consequently, local governments, citizen organizations, Chambers of Commerce and individual citizens began to consider what could be done to at least soothe the most insistent irritations. Many others have now learned the lesson which ACTION learned: that if you pick up one problem and start to unravel it, pretty soon you discover that the urban environment is all of one piece and you have the whole business in your hands. At this point the faint-hearted become discouraged and resign themselves to fate. The more stubborn and dedicated, as well as those who are fascinated by the complexity, push on to the generalization that a comprehensive approach is necessary.

Our good intentions are often blocked by focussing immediately upon the problems and insisting that something must be done soon. To understand the importance of comprehensive planning and dreaming let us ask ourselves what the potentialities are for the city. What could it become if we had the will and organization to create it? What are a few foresighted planners and architects already thinking? We become vaguely aware that any really imaginative proposal involves a wide range of fundamental questions which have not been raised in public discussion, let alone answered. We may originally ask how to alleviate our problems and inconveniences, but when we begin to move on the comprehensive scale which the problems demand, we gradually become aware that the original practical question has been transmuted into a philosophical inquiry. We must now ask what kind of city we want. We know what irritates. We do not know so well just what would satisfy us and give us pride in our community. We are a little embarrassed to discover that the question really is what we individually want to become and what kind of city is necessary to our growth.

When asking what a mature, interesting, and decent city is, we really ask what the good life should be in the seventh decade of the twentieth century. As Americans we pride ourselves in being a practical people—theoretical questions make us uncomfortable. We could avoid such questions while we were content to let the urban environment be the result of myriad private decisions with only a minimum of public participation. The realization that our problems can only be solved by planning on an unprecedented scale means that a whole range of values now become matters of social policy. Comprehensive planning means that we must find ways of expressing the moral, esthetic, educational, and political values of our citizens. For example, urban renewal, unlike the public housing program, is not merely a question of our responsibility for the poor and minority groups; more fundamentally it is a question of what both the middle class and the affluent expect out of life. We have the capacity to construct the urban environment to our heart's desire. But what do we desire?

If we are to mobilize public interest we must create an image of the future as well as an understanding of present frustrations. If we can translate what technology has made possible into social and cultural terms we will create a public opinion which may override many obstacles that now seem immovable.

2

The Future of the Metropolis

Our purpose is not to paint a picture of the ideal metropolis. There is no such single ideal pattern. Nationwide forces of various kinds may create some uniformities, but within them each metropolis has a different history, population, climate, economic base, and geographic setting. Within the same urban cluster there is an enormous variety of people. Our first premise is an acceptance of this variety. No single pattern will satisfy all groups. We must understand that the consumers of urban life are highly differentiated and that the ideal metropolis must be as variegated as its patrons. Our purpose here is to indicate some of the possibilities that now exist and to point out some of the value choices which are involved in guiding our metropolitan development. We cannot examine every aspect of urban life, but will limit our inquiry to the futures of housing, the neighborhood, and downtown.

HOUSING

One of the most unfortunate elements in our pattern of urban development since the end of World War II is the limited choice which has been provided the consumer of housing, especially new housing. The typical buyer of new housing was largely restricted in his choice to the available tract homes. If he had enough money he could build a house in an established suburb in the urban-rural fringe. If he had little money but chose to be a modern pioneer he could build his own house on the fringe, often living in the basement as he finished the house on a five- or ten-year basis.

The nature of tract developments usually meant that the buyer purchased housing and little else. It is not much of an exaggeration to say that the typical new home was located in the outlying areas without convenient public transportation, on a street yet to be paved, with a septic tank which would eventually need replacing by a sewer and sewage-treatment facilities, with a water system of uncertain long-run adequacy, with a graded but unfinished lot, without community recreational facilities, without adequate public health protection, with no shopping facilities within walking distance, with already overcrowded schools, and without adequate churches. The house itself was a single detached house.

This state of affairs is the result of a number of factors. First and most obvious is the fact that open land is beyond built-up facilities. Second, the building industry was the province of small-scale operators. They could buy a tract of land and begin putting up a few houses but they were not large enough to think about recreation, school, or commercial facilities. Third, the FHA seemed to have a preference for the detached house, particularly after they were embarrassed in the early Fifties by the Section 608 apartment-house scandals. Fourth, there was a lack of local planning in the new areas. There was no method of considering the over-all water needs, no planning for the full dimensions of the ultimate sewage problems, no providing for recreational space, and no integrating of the tracts' street system into an over-all highway plan. When zoning came it frequently took the form of forbidding "undesirable" uses. The latter often included industry and other good taxpayers.

The family in search of a home generally either had to accept this alternative with its built-in costs, present and future, or remain in the city with its aging housing supply, deteriorating neighborhoods, low-quality and often over-crowded schools, and insufficient open space for children. Many people, however, could not realistically select the second alternative because of the limited housing supply. It is fruitless to argue that the American people have a great preference for new tracts, that the new suburbs are the answer to a deep yearning for the country and the grass roots—millions had no choice but to move to the suburbs. We must provide real alternatives.

Already there are a number of hopeful signs. The scale of the building industry is on the increase. The FHA is once more encouraging apartments. Urban renewal is beginning to provide large, close-in tracts of land for housing development. Urban renewal is also just beginning to find out how to rehabilitate declining neighborhoods. Architects are beginning to reconsider such items as the row house. Subdivision planners are beginning to show some respect for the landscape and the quality of life the suburbs are supposed to engender. These are some of the items that suggest that the buyer or renter of the next decade may have more choice than his counterpart of the past 15 years.

However, we must begin to think about what is possible, about the enormous range and variety which technology and proper social organization could bring about if we demanded it. The main fact to keep in mind for the future is that there is no single housing market; there are rather a great many specialized markets.[1] No wonder commentators note with alarm the uniformity and conformity of our suburbs: their layouts express only an obsession with a geometric pattern which makes the planner's and surveyor's work easy. In addition, we have housing segregated by type and cost. This segregation is dictated by banking and FHA prejudices. The system tends to discourage rather than to encourage experimentation.

It is unfortunatly true that public opinion in many of our suburban towns and villages tends to discourage variety and experimentation. Many people have apparently succumbed to the argument that apartments and commercial development, let alone industry, depreciate the value of single-family dwellings. Consequently, in many places multiple residences and industry have been zoned out. Commercial development is confined to the shopping center, thus preventing more convenient shopping facilities. In fairness we should add that low-density suburbs do not have a sufficient population to support corner grocery stores. Too often a town adopts a zoning pattern copied from the ordinance of some adjacent town without really evaluating the peculiarities of its own situation.

To illustrate the enormously varied housing requirements of our

[1] We need more housing studies of the type done by Chester Rapkin and William G. Grigsby in *Residential Renewal in the Urban Core* (Philadelphia: University of Pennsylvania Press, 1960).

population, let us suggest the changing needs of the same individual or family from one stage of life to another.

When young people first get married many prefer apartment-dwelling. They are not yet ready for the responsibilities of home ownership. Many of them are not really capable of bearing the expense. Moreover, not all young people want the same kind of apartment. Some want a furnished apartment, especially if their first location is temporary. Others who prefer an unfurnished apartment take the first step toward home ownership by beginning to accumulate furniture, linen, silver, a car, and so on. Still others choose a garden-type apartment in relatively open country because they like peace and quiet. An apartment in the center of things with the activity, variety, and choice of the city appeals to some. Others prefer apartment-living on the edge of the country where recreational land is abundant. Different wants also depend upon whether the wife works or not.

Space needs certainly change with the coming of children. The suitability of locations may also change, but parenthood does not automatically create a desire for a detached single house in the suburbs. Not all parents enjoy the responsibility of home ownership, but too often it is the only way they can provide a good environment for their children.

When children reach school age the quality of school facilities becomes the center of concern. For many, perhaps most, this will be the time for moving to the suburbs. Yet many people will make the decision not so much in terms of the attractiveness of the new pattern but in terms of the unpleasantness of urban alternatives. We make a great mistake if we zone garden-type apartments out of existence in our suburbs, since many families with school-aged children prefer them. Some of these families will even prefer high-rise, or elevator apartments if the recreational problem is also solved. Some families will prefer a central location where they can escape the necessity of two cars and can be free to spend their money in some other way.

We need to consider measures which will reduce the tax advantage which home ownership enjoys over renting; mortgage interest charges and real estate taxes are deductions to the home owner on his federal income tax. One way is to encourage cooperative developments. Another way is to develop the principle of condominium which was incorporated in the Housing Act of 1961. Here the individual actually owns an individual apartment. He has rights in halls and open space and a financial obligation toward them. His apartment can be separately mortgaged and is easier to dispose of if he has to move than is a cooperative. The owner of a cooperative apartment in which he has a substantial equity often finds its difficult to find a buyer with sufficient cash. Suggestions have also been made for giving the renter the same tax treatment as the home owner. Such suggestions deserve exploration. A system should be sought to give the individual maximum freedom in selecting the way in which he shall live. There is no intrinsic superiority in home ownership. As long as the taxation system provides an arbitrary bonus for living in one way rather than another, freedom is curtailed.

It should be observed that families with children will increasingly want a separate summer home on the lake or in the country or mountains. It would appear that a home or apartment requiring minimum maintenance can be combined with this objective better than the suburban home on a large lot.

Different needs and desires may also develop when the children move from elementary school to high school. However, the next big point of change is apt to be the time when the children leave home to take a job, get married, or go to college. This is an especially critical matter in the coming decade and beyond. As the war and postwar babies reach maturity, millions of couples who moved to the suburbs for the sake of children will re-evaluate their situation as they once again become a pair in their late forties and fifties. We are going to need better facilities for these people than are now available in any abundance. Again, the main principle is that they should have a wide range of choice. Given such choice, many decide to stay where they are because they like what they have built. They want ample space so that their children can come home with the grandchildren on weekends, holidays and vacations. Some prefer a smaller house, but in a similar location. However, the smaller house they desire is apt to be different from the small house in which couples start out in life: they can afford more luxurious housing with better facilities and less skimping on space. Some prefer to move to a garden-type apartment, perhaps located away from the center of town. Again, however, this market may differ in quality and character of housing from the garden-apartment market for other age groups. Still others prefer to go back to the center of things. Already a boom in luxury apartments in the cities is getting under way. As the numbers in the age group which can afford luxury apartments increase rapidly in the years ahead the market will probably expand. Within this market for city apartments great variety of desires exist and no one pattern will suffice. Some prefer apartments located in a quiet residential setting but still conveniently close to the center of things, others prefer to have shops, stores, and restaurants available on the street below. Since still others prefer the town house, we can expect a great increase in demand for this kind of accommodation. If proper provision is made for sites one can confidently expect an increased building of row houses, many with enclosed courts. The experiences of Georgetown and similar places suggest a substantial market for rehabilitated luxury housing. For many, the emphasis will be upon a minimum of maintenance. As the do-it-yourself urge runs its course and the cost of hired help continues to rise, wise builders will concentrate on maintenance-free structures and grounds, particularly in town houses. This age group will doubtless require other kinds of choices not envisaged here. This is especially true when one realizes that many of the women involved will decide at this stage, or even earlier, to return to work. Apartments with built-in maid service may become very popular. In any case apartments which through design or service reduce the chores of housekeeping will be demanded. We may even have a boom in apartments featuring a central food service. Above all, the needs of this age group will require careful watching if we are to understand and meet their changing needs.

Increasingly, people in their late forties, fifties, and early sixties will probably need two homes to satisfy their needs. In some cases the second home will be comparable to the lake cottage already suggested for the younger group. For many, however, the process will be reversed. If the open country or the lake is not too far to drive to work, this may become the primary home. The secondary home may be a subleased apartment in town for the worst winter months. This becomes increasingly possible as the retired group leave their city apartments and go to Florida, California, or Arizona for the winter and sublet their northern apartments. One can even imagine, where location is favorable, the creation of apartment developments as the primary place of residence in a luxury resort atmosphere.

The last stage of life is retirement (although it too may be broken up by the death of one's partner or failing health). Certainly one of the main trends for retired folks will continue to be the trek south or west. Florida, California, and other places provide a wide variety of alternatives for retired couples or individuals. Although for many the cottage or small house is satisfactory, we should continue to experiment with other possibilities. More emphasis is now being given to the total environment than formerly. We are coming to recognize the special avocational, recreational, social, and cultural needs of older folks. However, we have only begun to scratch the surface of what is possible. For example, one is impressed with the great loyalty which many old folks have for Chautauqua. The symphony concerts, lectures, hobbies, recreation, bird-watching societies, book clubs, religious services, and pinochle enjoyed for the eight weeks of the season constitute for some of Chautauqua's summer residents the main reason for enduring the other 44 weeks of the year. The relative richness of the eight-week season at Chautauqua Institution only points up the general poverty of available choices.

Because of the pull of family, friends, and things familiar many retired folks desire to remain in the same area. We can expect the attraction of the city to be strong for many reasons. When one has a lot of free time it is desirable to have the range of choices which the city provides. Because we are getting tougher about permitting older people to drive cars, the public transportation system can be vital. For some the simple ritual of walking to the drugstore for a paper or tobacco is important. A hot lunch program for elderly shut-ins can be run in the city much more readily than in the suburbs or on the fringe.

In the city many old folks prefer to continue living in the same house or apartment which they occupied before retirement. They like the presence of young people and children and the sense of the familiar. The extra space is often important in order to encourage company. Some remain because no good alternative exists.

Others prefer to sell their house since much of the maintenance is now beyond them. Much deterioration in the city really results from the fact that the owner or occupant is growing old and lets upkeep slide. For some, especially when their partner dies, a downtown hotel may be a preferred location. In several cities hotels have been converted for occupancy by the aged.

Recognizing the need to provide a greater variety of choices for our older citizens, Congress in recent years has provided some special inducements to build housing for the elderly. Organized groups, such as teachers' organizations, are becoming aware of an opportunity for service in providing specialized housing for their retired members. The range of choice should be partly determined by differences in physical capacity. For those with no physical disability we need retirement houses and apartments in a variety of locations designed with the reduced capacity of the elderly in mind. For those who are ambulatory but in need of constant medical attention we need housing with some built-in medical facilities. For those who have largely lost the capacity to care for themselves we need more imaginative nursing homes.

Many prefer to be close to their children. In some instances, they can live in a room in the same house. Many prefer greater privacy, as do their children. We can expect an increase in houses built with a separate apartment for grandmother. Architects have not yet seriously devoted themselves to this problem. The zoning ordinance also often discourages this kind of development. We must modify our tendency to think that although the presence of grandmother in the spare bedroom is legitimate, providing her with greater space and privacy depresses values in the neighborhood.

One of the most interesting developments here is the rising use of the trailer. Part of the reason for it is economic, since retirement generally brings with it a substantial reduction in income. This kind of housing is relatively cheap, since the virtues of mass production have been most fully developed. It also has the advantage of minimizing maintenance problems. Trailers are sensible in warm climates where the restricted space of the trailer is expanded by an outdoor living area. A number of very attractive trailer courts have now been developed, some with a community hall and other common facilities. In warm climates, such as Palm Springs, the old folks in the hot weather may leave the trailer and make the rounds of the kids, friends, and relatives. In any case one may predict that trailers and trailer courts will become more luxurious, be better planned, provide more community facilities, and be generally more attractive and comfortable physically.

Many communities consider trailers a kind of blight and are trying to eliminate them. There is no doubt that planning and regulations are necessary.[2] A trailer court properly planned and controlled can be, however, an attractive, and for some people a desirable, place in which to live. It would appear the wiser course for the community to try to find the best use for this technologically-advanced housing rather than simply to ban it.

One of the drawbacks of trailer-living is that where it is used for housing families with children difficult taxation questions are raised. Also, the social desirability of raising children in such confined quarters is questionable. The community in planning the best location and use of trailers should bear in mind the desire (necessity in some cases) of many older folks to escape the heavy school taxes in districts with a large school-age population. Indeed, the almost universal advice given to older people of limited means is to move out of rapidly developing areas where the bill for improvements and schools is apt to be heavy.

One of the most important objectives in planning our urban environment is to furnish adequate housing. Therefore, any com-

[2] Some of the problems of regulating trailers are discussed by Stephen Sussna, "Trailers, Trailer Parks, and Zoning Cases," in *Urban Problems and Techniques*, No. 1, ed. Perry L. Norton (Lexington, Mass.: Chandler-Davis Publishing Co., 1959), pp. 217 ff.

munity that is trying to set goals for itself must undertake a housing inventory. First, it must discover what kinds of people inhabit it; how they are living; what the extent of deterioration is; what the situation is regarding over-occupancy; what kinds of people are having difficulty finding adequate housing within their means.

Second, and more difficult, the community should try to decide what an adequate housing supply would be. That a family has adequate accommodations and seems reasonably well satisfied is not proof that its needs have been met. We tend to judge the adequacy of what we have in terms of the desirability of the available alternatives. If our community provides a narrow range of alternatives our capacity for choice is limited. This difficulty is comparable to the public reaction to television. It is easy for an individual to say which of the available programs he likes best. It is not easy for him to say what he would like better until the alternative is actually created. Only when more housing alternatives are presented can we be sure that the hitherto unexpressed needs are fulfilled.

Third, the community must investigate ways of creating the additional alternatives required. When a few units of a new kind of housing are created, consumer demand will tell us how many more are needed; but the demand cannot be firmly expressed until the option exists. It is not our purpose here to discuss the gap between need and effective economic demand. The actual bridging of the gap, which involves housing subsidies of one kind or another, is a first priority of the community.

The large automobile companies rather belatedly thought that there were enough signs to justify producing the compact car. Neither they nor the public knew how many would be bought until the consumer was confronted with a choice. If we had not had foreign imports or such experimentation as the Rambler, the automobile industry might have gone on for a number of years before discovering that new uses and different, vaguely defined demands were developing. We are undergoing a similar alteration in housing. To overcome the inherent conservatism of the industry is much more difficult there than in the automobile industry. The habits of builders and architects, local custom and law, federal regulation, and the conservatism of financial interests—all interpose obstacles. A really determined effort will be required to create living opportunities which will satisfy the vague discontents now in the housing market. The fundamental principle is to forget about the average family and to talk about sub-markets for special kinds of people who are more diverse than the housing industry has yet realized.

THE NEIGHBORHOOD

The esthetic criticism of contemporary urban development is directed toward its sprawling, undifferentiated character. An aerial view of a city like Los Angeles reveals the regularity and the monotony of blocks stretching for miles in rectilinear fashion with one subdivision after another. There are no land marks or man-made monuments to orient him. He seems lost in a vast sea of sameness.

Even medium-sized urban areas are too large to permit a satisfying sense of communion with the whole. The individual needs a sense of involvement, participation, and affection for the parts as well as the whole. The parts which he knows best are his neighborhood, perhaps the place of his employment, and the specialized areas where he shops, is entertained, is spiritually and culturally elevated, finds recreation or perhaps is healed. When someone shows a visitor "his city" he does not drive him around at random. He picks out those features which are most distinctive and those which are sources of pride. In the past this has often meant individual buildings, but increasingly it is coming to mean certain specialized centers.

Our thinking about the city has been too much conditioned by the artificial categories of the zoning ordinance. It is most encouraging to observe the heightened interest in various kinds of urban clusters. There is relatively less talk about residential, commercial and industrial areas. In recent years we have heard a great deal about civic and cultural centers, about university cities and satellite towns, about medical and trade centers. We are even beginning to talk less about the central business district in the abstract and are beginning to think in terms of the smaller clusters of which it is composed. We hear of centers for office buildings, graphic arts, fashion, specialized retail shops, decorating, entertainment, and other kinds of clusters.

The shift of our focus from the individual building to a cohesive urban unit means that we can now design environments as well as buildings. The criteria of beauty can be employed in a more comprehensive way. In the wisest of our developments we also pay very close attention to the comfort and convenience of those who use the facilities. We can ask, for example, what auxiliary services and accommodations naturally go with a medical center. While the specialized units of the city give it much of its character, the quality of the city as an environment for living will be determined largely by the residential units. One finds a city delightful if the areas to which one goes to satisfy a wide range of human needs have their own pleasing identity and if his residential environment suits his peculiar needs.

The neighborhood may be conceived of as the area that can be conveniently traversed by foot from the home. It is the area of frequent face-to-face contact. It contains the elementary school and playground. It has the public and commercial facilities which adults require on a daily basis. The neighborhood unit as the critical element in city planning was introduced by Clarence A. Perry in 1929.[3] Perry's concept was built around an area large enough to include one elementary school. It was to be bounded by arterial streets, have its own small parks and recreational area as well as local shops. The schools and other neighborhood institutions were to be grouped together as the focal point of the neighborhood.

The enthusiasts for the neighborhood have devoted too much thought to the details of the ideal neighborhood. For example, a population of 5,000 is often cited as the optimum. However, there is no magic in such a figure. Nor is the ideal necessarily based on an elementary school of 600 pupils. Neighborhood design will vary both these numbers. Design is always a compromise between many values. There is no reason to take the most efficient unit of the ele-

[3] Clarence Arthur Perry, "The Neighborhood Unit," *Regional Survey of New York and its Environs*, Vol. VII (New York: Regional Plan Association, 1929), pp. 34-35.

mentary school as the controlling value. We may decide to suffer a little inefficiency in this regard, and perhaps have a school for 300 pupils, in order to achieve certain other values.

The main objective to be sought in neighborhood design is the elimination of the restraints imposed upon imagination by the practices of lending institutions, the FHA, zoning ordinances, subdivision regulations, the propensity to segregate rental properties from owner-occupied homes and our tendency to segregate by socio-economic status. This is not to argue that these restraints always result in undesirable developments, it is only to say that they needlessly limit the choices which are available.

It is clear that the city will not fall into an orderly series of neighborhoods based on the elementary school. Inevitably the high school and the larger shopping areas serve a broader area. Consequently from these broader service areas the concept of community planning developed. The community was composed of a number of neighborhood units. For example, Manhattan is divided into twelve community planning districts.[4] Other cities have used larger or smaller units. The need is to break up the large urban mass into units which are manageable for planning purposes and which correspond to the individual's sense of identification and participation. We will not be able to find any unit which is wholly satisfactory. The neighborhood unit, the urban community, the city and the metropolitan area as well as other units for particular purposes can all have meaning and vitality in specific ways. For effective planning we undoubtedly need an area larger than the neighborhood unit. Yet it is useful to think of the community unit as being composed of neighborhoods.

The neighborhood can be thought of as being bounded by arterial streets or other barriers as well as containing basic services. In recent years the principle of creating a relatively large area from which vehicles are barred has been advanced as the basis for a neighborhood unit.

The main exponent in recent years of the principle that vehicular

[4] Martin B. Dworkis, ed., *The Community Planning Boards of New York* (New York: New York University Graduate School of Public Administration, 1961).

traffic should be separated from pedestrian traffic has been Victor Gruen. This idea received its first major expression in Gruen's plan for downtown Fort Worth.[5] However, others including Clarence Perry and Richard Neutra had earlier suggested the same principle for the neighborhood. Neutra wanted to return the neighborhood to the pedestrian.[6] He seems to have the city neighborhood in mind.

Except, perhaps, in suburban developments with large lots, the tendency to think of the metropolitan neighborhood unit in terms of the pedestrian is probably sound. The elements which give the neighborhood cohesion are the school, library, church, convenience-shopping, recreational, and local assembly facilities. They can be variously located and combined. Some neighborhoods will want other features, such as restaurants, taverns, pool halls, laundromats, and soda fountains. It is this variation in the cohesive elements which gives the neighborhood much of its distinctive character.

The design of the dwellings and their relation to each other influence the balance between privacy and social intercourse. The desire for intimacy varies. It may be especially important for children and older folks because of their restricted mobility. Some people may prefer to select their friends from across the city, or even the nation, and, therefore, prefer protection from the demands of neighborliness.

One way of thinking about the desired diversity is to relate land use to the transportation system. We have already suggested the desirability of some apartment developments. There is no reason, except because of inadequate local planning, why apartment developments should not be concentrated along major lines of transportation. The developments can start in the city and spread out to the suburbs. The aim is to provide a sufficient concentration of population to support the system of public transportation. Our pattern of urban diffusion automatically destroys public transportation, since the population is too thin. If some people desire to live in apartments and at least free themselves from the necessity

[5] Victor Gruen has best stated his position in "The Emerging Urban Pattern," *Progressive Architecture,* July, 1959.

[6] Richard Neutra, *Survival Through Design* (New York: Oxford University Press, 1954).

of the second car, then it would be wise social policy to construct our zoning ordinances to provide both the concentration which mass transit requires and the diffusion which the car makes possible. People ought to be able to locate where there is at least good transportation to the main shopping center, the primary places of employment and the concentration of professional, social, and cultural services. We cannot expect adequate public transportation to the more sparsely settled residential areas. In our medium-sized and small cities we should abandon certain areas to the private automobile but in other areas seek a greater concentration of activity in order to justify improved public transportation. Especially in our medium-sized cities a conscious policy of concentration is necessary if we are to reverse the cycle of higher bus fares, fewer riders, reduction in schedules, more losses, and so back to higher fares. In many small cities public transportation may be doomed. Preservation of mass transit is especially important for the poor, some of whom we still have with us, and the older folks, of whom we shall have a great many more.

Even in the new subdivisions which are based upon the automobile greater variety is possible.[7] For example, there is no reason that apartments and detached houses should not be integrated into one neighborhood, perhaps built around the shopping center. The design could encourage walking to the shopping and service center. Most of our shopping centers do not even have sidewalks connecting them to nearby residential areas. There should be room for both the pedestrian and the car. In coming years we will doubtless have further experimentation, building clusters of apartments with shops and stores on the ground floor. There is no reason for apartments and shops not to face each other across a central pedestrian mall with parking below or to the rear on both sides. Indeed the new shopping centers are deserting the long strip development in favor of shops facing each other across such a pedestrian mall. A few are even enclosing and air conditioning the central mall. This is especially important in northern climates, as demon-

---

[7] Richard A. Miller has an interesting discussion of the present state of the art of subdividing in "The Slumberous State of Subdivision Planning," *Architectural Forum*, February, 1959, pp. 99 ff.

strated by the Southdale development outside Minneapolis. Some of these shopping centers might well have apartments above and pedestrian access to the surrounding neighborhood. The concept of the shopping center is beginning to broaden into a genuine center. Recreational activities, offices, libraries, and even churches are increasingly being included. It may be that before long schools and shopping centers will be planned together.

Local zoning ordinances in suburban areas have greatly restricted the imagination of builders.[8] If given greater freedom, they might well construct far more imaginative and practical developments on their own initiative. Some builders, for instance, hold the theory that the two-story row house has some great advantages for the new subdivision. Basically the plan is to build clusters of row houses around the perimeter of the subdivision. In general the row houses face each other across little courts, with enclosed patios in the rear. Cars are parked at the entrance to the courts. The dwellings are clustered close together, thus reducing street construction, sewer, and water costs. In the center of the development is a large recreational area, accessible to the whole development without the crossing of a single street. The over-all density is not greater than that of many subdivisions. This plan concentrates the open space into one large usable area instead of distributing a few thousand square feet to each house, as is conventionally done. It is a more economical design than the usual pattern, having more privacy in spite of closer physical proximity, and more usable open space. It provides less opportunity for the free-wheeling gardener and less, although adequate, space for small tots who require watching from the window. For some people, at least, the advantages probably outweigh the disadvantages.

Other builders have suggested using smaller lots and donating the saved space for a common golf course. We need trials in these directions in order to determine the demand. In many areas zoning laws will require revision in order to permit experimentation. Also

[8] For an excellent discussion of the most imaginative residential developments built in the United States, see Clarence S. Stein, *Toward New Towns for America* (New York: Reinhold Publishing Corporation, 1957).

we need a more enlightened policy on the matter of maintaining and supervising such recreation areas. Already we have discovered that a city-planning commission with extra-territorial jurisdiction may try to require a subdivider beyond the city limits to provide recreational space, only to discover that the government of the town in which the subdivision is located refuses to accept the playground, because it would have to maintain it.

Other planners have called for a greater integration of the place of work and the residence. In this direction we are beginning to get some combination hotels and office buildings and in a few instances a combination of apartments with offices. However, what the planners often have in mind is the residence and the factory. Certainly the new style of much factory construction opens the door for residences nearby. The factory, like the commercial district, is not automatically a blighting influence. The man walking to work can leave his wife at home with freedom of movement, rather than confined and trapped as is so often the case unless they can afford two cars. Again experimentation is required before we can discover the market potential.

Neighborhoods variously composed of single-family homes, apartment buildings, a mixture of apartments and homes, mixed residential and commercial use, mixed residential, industrial and commercial use; neighborhood based upon the car and others upon mass transit; neighborhoods oriented around a variety of focal points; neighborhoods both loosely and tightly integrated with variously composed populations—all are necessary in every metropolitan area in order to provide freedom of choice. Each metropolitan area should also have a distinctive series of specialized centers which serve areawide needs. In the end the market will decide what kinds of neighborhoods and specialized units are most congenial to human survival and development.

DOWNTOWN

The central core, or downtown, has much reason for continued existence. It is not an accident that Wall Street concentrates so much of the nation's business and financial leadership in such a small area. The desirability of easy contact between many related functions is the fundamental reason for the shopping, commercial, and financial concentrations which characterize our cities. After World War II a number of businesses experimented with moving their offices to the suburbs. On the whole this has not been sufficiently successful to suggest the functional obsolescence of downtown. The enormous office boom now going on in Manhattan suggests the continued vitality of intense concentrations of activity.

There are many reasons why downtown is not so easily diffused. Modern business is a highly complex affair requiring a wide variety of talents and resources including administrative, financial, legal, insurance, advertising, and others. Easy face-to-face communication is essential if the executive is to keep abreast of rapid business developments. The business luncheon is a vital part of the exchange of ideas which is so important to the executive. On a different level it is much easier to assemble the office staff in the downtown location. A number of insurance companies have discovered that the outlying location has increased the clerical turnover because noontime shopping facilities are meager or non-existent. A modern office also requires a lot of servicing more readily available downtown.

Although downtown shopping centers have not been growing much in recent years, they have still another important reason for existence. Downtown, the variety and choice, particularly of luxury items, is necessarily much greater. Downtown will probably continue to decline for convenience shopping, but as we become wealthier and our tastes ever more differentiated, downtown comparison shopping will grow unless we permit it to become inaccessible. The suburban shopping centers devoted to shopper convenience will continue to grow, although by their nature they cannot provide the range of selection available downtown.

Historically, downtown has been a concentration of related activities. That character will continue, but with some changes. Wholesaling, light manufacturing, convenience shopping, and certain facilities such as doctors' offices have been moving away from the

central core.[9] However, public administration, business headquarters, legal and insurance services, financial institutions, sales
and advertising services, entertainment, and differentiated shopping
comprise a cluster, or a series of related clusters, which draw
strength from each other.

The major threat to this cluster has been the automobile. If the
automobile becomes a nuisance and tends to distort many of the
pleasures and purposes of life in our residential neighborhoods
it threatens the very existence of our downtown areas. It has often
been observed that 85 per cent of the land area in downtown Los
Angeles is devoted to the automobile in one way or another. Consequently, Los Angeles, a new city without a real center, is a hor-
rible example of what the car can do to the city. Reliance upon
the automobile results in exorbitant demands for highway and parking space. This makes it impossible to achieve that concentration
of related activities traditionally associated with the center of cities.
Victor Gruen has estimated that total dependence upon the automobile in Manhattan would necessitate devoting the first nine
stories of all structures to transportation space.[10] Offices and stores
would have to start at the tenth story. We know that new shopping
centers often provide four or five times as much parking space as
floor area inside the structures. This parking space does not include
the associated streets to handle the traffic. Adequate zoning of new
office structures located so that they depend primarily upon the
automobile often requires a good deal more parking space than
office-floor space. Business or functional convenience has in some
instances been overbalanced by the congestion, lack of parking
space and time lost in traffic snarls.

Consequently, most proposals to revitalize downtown have been
directed at the automobile. One proposal is that only a reinvigor-
ated mass-transit system and a reduced reliance upon the auto-

[9] These trends are discussed in Raymond Vernon, *The Changing Economic
Function of the Central City* (New York: Committee for Economic Development, 1959).

[10] Victor Gruen, "The Emerging Urban Pattern," *Progressive Architecture*, July,
1959, p. 128. Gruen further contends that even then the parking problem would
not be solved.

mobile can save downtown. For our larger cities this is certainly true. For them an answer to the transit problem is imperative.

Many cities could have provided marvelous systems of mass transportation if they had spent their highway funds on public rather than private transportation. However, such a choice was not available. State, and especially federal, subsidies have been available for highways but not for subways or better bus systems. Federal highway funds, probably in excess of 20 billion dollars, are to be spent in urban areas under the inter-state highway program. The increased congestion in our cities is apparently considered important to the national defense. Providing a balanced system for the movement of goods and people is conversely considered unimportant to the national defense. So, at least, the subsidy system says. The local community is not free to use the tax dollars according to some other sensible plan, if it chooses. Ninety per cent of the cost of the highways is borne by the federal government and 10 per cent by the state. The metropolitan area does not even decide whether the highway shall be built. It is certainly not the metropolis' right to decide whether building highways constitutes the top priority for the city or the national defense. However, San Francisco has even considered tearing up the expressway already started in that city because many felt that to complete it would be a disaster. The increased use of the private automobile which has resulted from highway construction has brought many mass-transportation systems to the point of crisis, threatened to strangle the downtown street system, and thrown a huge parking burden upon business and government.

Even our middle-sized and smaller cities have cause to be concerned about the private car. Many of them can probably solve their problems even if a fairly high percentage of their people come to the central business district by car. What they must be concerned with is the spiral of declining patronage and declining service which eventually bankrupts the public transportation system. In most places the cycle is already under way. Unless it is reversed or at least halted what now appears a soluble problem may become insoluble. A subsidy system, as well as a land-use system, must be developed which will encourage the use of public rather than private transportation. The process of subsidizing only the highways breeds further use of them and renders them inadequate soon after they are completed. The highways on the whole are good; it is the national policy of destroying competing modes of travel that is objectionable.

The other solution to the problems of the core area which has been advanced is to separate pedestrian from vehicular traffic. While the improvement of mass transit is intended to prevent strangulation of downtown, the principle of developing pedestrian islands in the city aims at making the city genuinely more attractive and pleasant. The idea of a pedestrian central business district began to be discussed seriously when Gruen developed his plan for Fort Worth: to ring the downtown area with superhighways. From this inner loop one could enter a series of parking garages which reached into the interior of the central business district. Any place downtown could be reached by the pedestrian in two and one-half minutes from some garage exit. Traffic within the core would be divided into two levels. The upper level would be exclusively pedestrian. One could move from store to store or from office to restaurant along pleasant landscaped areas without the noise and irritation of vehicular traffic. There would be some small, slow, electrical carts for those who have difficulty in walking. The lower level would provide access by public transportation and for servicing the downtown core. It is this dream of converting downtown into a pleasant pedestrian island which has seized the contemporary imagination.

Victor Gruen and Herbert Askwith have even gone so far as to suggest applying the zoning principle to vehicular traffic in Manhattan.[11] Private automobiles would, in general, be restricted to the periphery. Other areas would be open to buses, taxis, and trucks during certain hours. Still other areas would become pedestrian islands. The most dramatic proposal is to restrict cross-town traffic and convert Fifth Avenue from Thirty-fourth Street to Fifty-ninth Street into a pedestrian plaza. Without attempting to judge the feasibility of this proposal, one can readily see that the adoption of

[11] Victor Gruen and Herbert Askwith, "Plan to End Our Traffic Jam," *New York Times Magazine*, January 10, 1960, pp. 18 ff.

such a proposal would convert Fifth Avenue into an even more fabulous window-shopping area than it is now. Modest landscaping plus some benches for resting would make the avenue an even more powerful magnet.

Gruen is to be congratulated for insisting that these dreams are practical. He is aware that in most instances it will take a long time to realize them and that in many instances compromises will be required. This does not vitiate his main point that a city should have a goal for its development and that the concept of the pedestrian zone provides one important goal. Probably close to 100 cities are now considering some kind of mall or plaza, not all of them, unfortunately, well conceived. It is seldom simply a matter of closing off a few blocks of downtown in order to allow new life to flourish. Unless the related traffic and parking problems are adequately considered a city can generate a whole new set of difficult problems. Integrating new pedestrian space into the environment is sometimes given inadequate attention. Most important is the necessity of making the move a part of a total plan for revitalizing the downtown area. In the end it will be up to merchants and other businessmen to make the move successful. Old buildings need to be remodelled and spruced up. Some buildings are beyond salvage and need to be torn down in order to provide room for new growth at the very heart of the city.

There are several dangers in the emphasis upon plazas. One is that the plaza becomes an end in itself: the bigger the better. It should be remembered that the purpose of the pedestrian island is to facilitate the individual's shopping, business transactions, or search of food and pleasure. Downtown is not a park. The purpose of the pedestrian island is to make possible a more intense use of the land and to bring into the smallest possible geographic area that cluster of inter-related activities which makes downtown both convenient and exciting. The street is of primary importance, because it is along the street that merchants display their wares, and other temptations beckon. The street and the elevator are the threads which connect one activity with another. The end sought is not so much to beautify the plaza as to facilitate pedestrian movement from shop to shop or from one activity to another.[12]

Another danger of the plaza concept is that suburban ideals will thereby be transplanted to the city. Open space downtown should be used very sparingly. Too much open space increases walking distances. As a general rule, it should be spread around in small plots. Although modest landscaping enhances the scene, shrubbery should not be permitted to dominate. Downtown, the shop windows and the buildings are the center of attention; we should not be ashamed of them but accentuate them.

It should also be emphasized that developments appropriate to California are not necessarily appropriate everywhere. In California the out-of-doors is pleasant most of the year and one passes comfortably from the shop to the street or plaza. We should not forget that one of the basic purposes of revitalizing downtown is comfort. Consequently, in northern areas the flowers and shrubs should not only be placed behind the shop windows in priority, but also behind comfort. Therefore, protecting the individual from the severe winter weather becomes a prime consideration. Again the best shopping centers point the way. Southdale outside Minneapolis makes it possible to utilize the entire shopping center in air-conditioned comfort. In many northern areas this, rather than an attractive outdoor plaza which is pleasant only a few months of the year, should be the prime consideration. The ideal should be to make it possible for the individual, at least in a medium-sized city, to have all the facilities of downtown at his disposal in shirt-sleeved comfort even in the winter time. Although this ideal will be a long time coming, it is more basic than open-air plazas which serve as funnels for the winter's wind. We should begin connecting our buildings by air-conditioned sidewalks or arcades. In warm climates they can perhaps be open-air, but even here we should be aware of the need for protection from the summer heat.

Our ultimate goal for small and medium-sized cities should be to make it possible for the individual to drive his car downtown

[12] William H. Whyte, Jr. has discussed some of the dangers arising from urban redevelopment in "Come to the Aid of the City," originally published in *Encounter* and republished in *Best Articles and Stories*, October, 1959.

and leave his coat and overshoes in the car at the parking garage so that he may enjoy in comfort the air-conditioned downtown complex. The mass transit system should also provide lockers in the downtown terminal where winter clothes can be checked. Simply providing a pleasant place for the shopper to rest for a moment is one of the little things that make a great deal of difference.

The shopping center is a clustering of convenience goods and necessities. Downtown should constitute a group of sub-clusters which are close enough together for easy movement from one to another. The most pronounced trend in this direction is the grouping of governmental buildings now being planned in many communities as civic or cultural centers. We should also encourage a kind of private coordination now too rare in our cities. The Greater Boston Economic Study Committee suggests the desirability of developing in Boston a graphic arts center, a women's apparel center, and a decorative arts center.[13] Downtown will be attractive for comparison shopping if we make the process convenient. Someone interested in women's apparel should not have to travel all over the central business district in order to have effective choice. Such concentrations already exist in some places to some extent. We should push the process even further and attempt to plan more units including office buildings, theaters, restaurants, furniture dealers, jewelers, men's clothing and others. However, in pursuing the goal of building distinctive clusters we should not let our enthusiasm exclude other considerations, for example, it is obviously desirable to have restaurants and some other facilities convenient to all parts of downtown. Yet some clustering can aid the person who wants to choose. The objective is to maximize the convenience of the individual in transacting the kinds of business which brings him downtown, including the pursuit of pleasure.

Let us take one other example to illustrate the different tastes which are developing and suggest the vitality which particularized clusters can have. Most shopping centers have one or two supermarkets and perhaps a bakery and almost certainly a liquor store with a basic stock. Today many people are experimenting in their

[13] *A Report on Downtown Boston* (Boston: Greater Boston Economic Study Committee, 1959).

food consumption. No longer is a basic wholesome meal the limit of the housewife's aspiration. She likes to try strange and exotic foods. Preferences are often developed for certain national dishes. While the supermarket provides more choice than the old corner grocery, the choice is still limited. The housewife's (sometimes it is the husband's) desire for culinary experimentation is restricted by the inconvenience of having to travel all over town in order to find the rare foods and condiments required. Consequently, there is developing in most metropolitan areas the need for a highly diverse and sophisticated food shopping center, different from that found in the suburbs. In such a center we would find not only the supermarket staples, but the widest selection of fresh fruits and vegetables, nationality bakeries and butcher shops, health foods, all manner of imported foods, spices and beverages, which the searching American palate now desires. Such centers might be built close to downtown, particularly if an urban renewal site were available, since it should be conveniently located for the whole metropolitan area. Several such centers, of course, could be supported in our larger cities.

OTHER GOALS

Possibilities for the future have been discussed in terms of housing, the neighborhood, and downtown. These items were selected in order to highlight some of the planning elements that are often inadequately considered. They are not the kind of issues which often get raised in public discussion. Our intention was not to slight the more traditional questions. Making the city more attractive and desirable should certainly start with the very basic considerations. A great many cities would be greatly improved by the mere process of keeping the streets clean and in good repair, by improving the law-enforcement processes, and by a more efficient system of garbage and rubbish pick-up. Some of our cities are now finding it necessary to eliminate great numbers of diseased trees, particularly elms. A policy requiring a new planting for each tree removed would prevent the denuding of the city. Many cities could provide more adequate playground space and make better use of what they already have. Our educational standards and ideals seem to have slipped in many cities. Many of our city schools are grossly inadequate in facilities, curriculum, and staff. The city has often lost to the suburbs much of the middle-class leadership upon which the quality of the school depends. We need to recapture some of this urban leadership for the sake of a healthy public school system. Conversely, attracting it back depends upon the schools in many instances.

In general we should ask ourselves what kind of life our children, our teenagers, our married couples, and our older folks would like to lead if the choices were available. For every stage of life and income group the question should be what "the good life" can be for them in the latter part of the twentieth century. Only when we get a picture of the changing and varied nature of the good life will we be able clearly to formulate the economic, educational, social, and cultural goals of our development. Our dream for the future of the metropolis is one of subtle and striking variety, of differentiated tastes and opportunities.

3

The Context of National Forces

In order to understand the potentialities and problems of the city and its metropolitan area we must realize the extent to which its fate is determined by forces that are national and even international in scope. The city is a microcosm, subject to the technological, economic, social, and political forces of the greater society.[1] The potentialities of the city will be determined by the university and industrial research laboratory, the national financial system, the policies of national corporations concerning their community responsibilities, the ethical standards of the International City Managers' Association and other such groups, the policy of the American Institute of Architects regarding the building module, the policies of the Housing and Home Finance Agency, and other social welfare policies. Our changing concept of the requirements of the equalitarian ideal, the content we choose to give to the ideal of liberty, our national attitudes toward family size, and a host of other factors also limit local choice.

TECHNOLOGY

We may be certain that new technology will have an enormous impact on our metropolitan areas. One is impressed not only with the fact of technological change but even more with the acceleration of the process. Perhaps the greatest challenge to the city is the need to develop our social,

[1] Probably the best general discussion of the changes that are occurring in America is found in A. W. Zelomek, *A Changing America* (New York: John Wiley & Sons, Inc., 1959).

economic, and political institutions rapidly enough to convert technological largess into a blessing rather than a curse. Social policy, of course, determines to some extent the areas in which technological progress will occur. It has been many decades, for instance, since we have had much innovation in our systems of public transportation; the bus was its last great invention. Our economic system has not been geared to encourage invention in public transportation. Our political policy has not provided substitute incentives. We need a mechanism both for encouraging technological development in this area and for experimenting with developments as they occur. A declining industry is reluctant to undertake large new capital expenditures when other forces in the society seem bent upon destroying it.

Urban concentration and public transportation have been in a destructive cycle for some time. It is likely that we are about to move into a period of greater urban concentration in some of our new developments and, consequently, to develop a healthier environment for public transportation. Public policy can help by eliminating some of the existing tax burdens, which are no longer justifiable since the monopoly advantage of the transit system has been destroyed by competition from the private car. We can also help by using zoning to re-enforce the transit system, and by encouraging research. It can easily be argued that the various levels of government should pay public transportation a subsidy in order to reduce the governments' total transportation expenditures. A small subsidy for public transportation in some instances would eliminate the need of large highway expenditures. From the standpoint of the local community, preserving the public transportation system may partially prevent taking more and more valuable land off the tax rolls for the construction of highways and parking spaces. Every level of government must give its attention to this problem in order to reverse the balance of forces which has been running so heavily in favor of the private car since the end of World War II.

In spite of the hopes which we may have for public transportation we may safely predict that the pattern of urban sprawl made possible by the automobile will continue. Our population will keep on growing at the rate of approximately three million per year. By the end of the next decade our absolute growth will be even more rapid unless our attitude toward family size changes again. Most of this growth continues to be in the metropolitan areas. A portion of the growth may be absorbed through more intensive land use in the built-up areas of our cities, but most of it will of necessity occur in the outlying areas. However, as state and local controls regarding sewage disposal and water supply become more stringent and as the population comes to demand more and better facilities, the economics of site purchase and development, plus the economy of large-scale development, will further accelerate the existing trend toward industrialization of the housing industry. It is hoped that the housing industry will experiment with new kinds of development less profligate in the consumption of new land than the existing pattern. Regional planning will be necessary to encourage such experimentation. The development of new building materials and the preassembly of units will continue to reduce labor and maintenance costs. The shortage of land may lead to the reversal of the trend toward the single-story school and factory. A modest change in school design is already imminent in order to conserve land. The two and three story school will return where land is expensive, both to reduce land costs, and to keep as much land as possible for recreation. The multi-story factory could return if the means were found for reducing material-handling costs.

We shall probably see further development of parking facilities adjacent to the mass transit system. The revolution in our car-buying habits suggests a great willingness to buy cars for special purposes. The diffused pattern of development makes mass transit impossible unless people drive some distance by car to a collecting and distributing point on the transit system. This is an expensive way to get to work, especially if it means a second car to park at the station, but many feel the gains of suburban life warrant it.

Parking will continue to be one of our pressing downtown problems. Continued experimentation will certainly be necessary in order to move the shopper and office worker rapidly from parking lots along the highway system to the core of the city. Shuttle buses are already in use in some places. Perhaps some city will try moving sidewalks for this purpose. Our desire is to prevent too much of the land in the urban core from being consumed by parked or moving cars. We need experimentation with quick, cheap systems of public transportation for this special purpose. More attention should be devoted to subsidizing experiments. Research is fine in its way, but a demonstration project is necessary at some point.

Some city may attempt to solve the problem by building several layers of parking under the whole downtown core. In some cases this could be done with underground parking, in others it might be necessary to raise the street level to the third or fourth story. The private car will continue to receive great consideration downtown especially in our metropolitan areas of less than a million inhabitants, and in some of the larger ones. In the largest cities the trend will probably be to find ways of excluding the car, perhaps following Gruen's plan for Manhattan.

We need a better way of relating science and technology to urban development. The irritating problem of exhaust fumes illustrates the difficulty of this relationship. It seems most critical to California, which has decided to adopt some standard of exhaust abatement. California will be followed by other states which may develop different requirements. Such variety of standards could create problems for the manufacturer. In the absence of a national standard he does not know what degree of abatement to ask his researchers to achieve. We need a mechanism for setting a minimum national standard which will then encourage a uniform widespread solution. The Council of State Governments may be the agency for developing a model state law. The difficulty is that the Council is not set up to do research on a national scale on such technical problems. It may become necessary to impose the standard at the federal level. Similarly, the building industry faces now a search for new materials which should be intensified. From their point of view the difficulty is the system of local code adoption and enforcement. Local enforcement agencies do not have the research staff to determine, for example, the fire resistance of a new product. The manufacturer cannot be sure how much of the national market will be permitted to use his new material. Again we need a national system of clearance in order to get the benefits of mass production and encourage research.

As important as these matters are, a more basic one remains. This issue can be suggested by an analogy with research for national defense. We do not leave the matter of defense research solely to private industry. We have professional military men and government scientists whose job it is to project our weapons requirements, to identify the inventions that will be needed to meet the requirements, and to suggest the lines of basic research which may produce the inventions. Knowing that a more powerful rocket fuel is required for national defense and that certain basic questions need answering in order to develop the fuel, the government supports the basic research. The point here is that we have a group of men trying to identify the fundamental questions to be answered before practical inventions are possible. A similar mechanism is needed to tackle the problems of the city. Administrators, planners, engineers, and scientists should be brought into a more fruitful relationship. The technological issues must be formulated and the basic problems identified, to encourage the research that is beyond the capacity of private industry.

A difficult additional problem remains—the problem of experimentation. An automobile manufacturer develops a new car, builds a few models and subjects them to exhaustive tests. Cities, however, are reluctant to build a new type of transit system which experience may demonstrate to have basic flaws. In many directions the processes of trial and demonstration are blocked because it is not in the interest of any one city to be "guinea pig." We should perhaps develop a subsidy system to encourage a few cities to experiment boldly with new technology. A precedent exists in agriculture's demonstration farms and the demonstration grants provided in the Housing Act. However, demonstration grants in housing are available only for modest purposes. They were a partial compensation for the action of an ill-advised Congress when it eliminated the research arm of the Housing and Home Finance Agency. The decision of the HHFA to spend a large portion of its new transportation appropriation on demonstration projects is a good beginning.

It becomes very difficult to gauge the potential impact of inventions which have not yet been tried by American cities, such as the monorail, or of potential inventions such as a heliocar.[2] Such items will probably have little effect in the next ten or fifteen years, but beyond that it is hazardous to project.

ECONOMIC FORCES

The most critical local problem which national economic forces have instigated is a crisis in local leadership, often the consequence of nationalizing careers. National concerns have been absorbing local manufacturing, merchandising, and banking firms at a rapid rate in recent years. This has been paralleled by the growing importance of the national level in labor organizations, health agencies such as the Heart or Cancer Fund, and professional organizations. Thus, the locally-employed engineer or business executive, as well as labor official, interprets success as promotion to headquarters in New York, Chicago, or Washington. The town he happens to be located in is a temporary home and his frequent moves discourage involvement in the local community. Rapidly disappearing is the local merchant prince with a deep commitment to the community. Such men were at the apex of a clearly defined community power structure. However, the occupational character of continuing local leadership has been shifting. The relative importance of lawyers, heads of insurance agencies, public relations men, real estate people, and such franchise businessmen as automobile dealers has increased as that of the older business types has declined. Power and wealth are less concentrated than formerly. The diffusion of power perhaps opens the door for more democratic citizen organization, but in many instances the natural leaders have been eliminated. Moreover, the lack of a clearly defined power structure inhibits the capacity for action and increases the number of points at which action can be blocked. The representatives of national organizations tend to be preoccupied with the national hierarchy. In any case their relatively short tenure means that even the active ones are often trans-

___

[2] For an imaginative view of future possibilities in transportation, including the airmobile, see Wilfred Owen, "Transportation," *The Annals of the Academy of Political and Social Science,* November, 1957, pp. 30-38.

ferred just as they have acquired competence on the local scene.

This difficulty extends into the lower levels of social organization, for it is not only top management who is moved but engineers and middle management as well. Consequently, parent-teacher organizations, churches, the Boy Scouts, and social agencies must subsist on a narrower margin of continuing leadership.[3]

Some corporations have recently become conscious of this problem and are encouraging their staff to participate more actively in community affairs. On the whole this is a healthy, even necessary, development. One way to accomplish this has been to institutionalize the corporation's relation to the community by appointing a public relations or community relations officer. This device has probably been most successful in support of the Community Chest. In this area most large corporations are good citizens: their employees work on the drive and the corporation supports it with funds. However, a public or community relations officer cannot substitute for the active participation of the principal managers, particularly in new areas of need which have not yet been institutionalized. Thus the political party, metropolitan area, urban renewal, juvenile delinquency, housing problems, and policy formation generally have been deprived of much of the community's leadership potential. Some corporations are now tackling these sensitive areas.[4] In a few instances the process of promotion may take into account this kind of activity as well as more business-oriented factors. This is all to the good, although the turn-over in personnel still constitutes a stumbling-block.

Perhaps the greatest issue in connection with this new sense of social responsibility on the part of business is the perspective with which the corporation views its involvement. The problem is illuminated by an examination of Sears, Roebuck and Company and the General Electric Company, two of the pioneers in this field. Their differences in approach arise from differing degrees of understand-

---

[3] The failure of the lower echelons to assume civic and political responsibilities is discussed by Norton E. Long in "The Corporation, Its Satellites, and the Local Community," *The Corporation in Modern Society*, ed. Edward S. Mason (Cambridge: Harvard University Press, 1960).

[4] "Corporations Make Politics Their Business," *Fortune*, December, 1959, pp. 100 ff.

ing of the nature of the problems and from differing conceptions of the nature of their stake in the problems.

Sears, Roebuck and Company has conducted an enlightened customer relations program for many years. It has originated or supported many activities beneficial to the farmer. For example, early in this century it provided a subsidy to counties willing to hire an agricultural expert who would provide help and guidance to the county's farmers. In a few years the Federal Government adopted the program, and introduced the County Agent. Sears' approach was to promote activities which were genuinely in the interest of their customers. The hope of course was that the resulting goodwill would pay off in a greater volume of business. The record of the company suggests that they were correct.

Several years ago Sears reappraised its customer relations program in the light of the changed nature of their business. Three quarters of its business is now done by the urban retail outlets. Sears decided that the best thing it could do was to ally itself with the urban renewal program. Self-interest was instrumental in selecting this approach. Sears has two kinds of direct interest in urban renewal. First, a clean up, fix up, paint up campaign would stimulate demand for many of the products they sell. Second, they have a number of stores in deteriorating areas. They were experiencing difficulty with these locations. Shoplifting was a problem. High quality labor tended to avoid some locations. Some Sears customers were sufficiently repelled by the neighborhoods to take their business elsewhere. In some instances it came to the point where Sears was confronted with the choice of abandoning its investment in the location or of attempting to do something about the neighborhood. Therefore, Sears' support of urban renewal is firmly rooted in its self-interest.

Sears' first major step was to acquaint its own personnel with the urban renewal program. To this end it published a very professional booklet entitled *The ABC's of Urban Renewal*. Intended primarily for the education of Sears employees, it was such an objective and competent job that the public demand for it was enormous. Originally 10,000 copies were printed. Within two years almost 100,000 copies had been distributed in spite of Sears' attempt to cut down requests for multiple orders. Sears' second major effort was an equally excellent booklet entitled *Citizens in Urban Renewal*. This booklet provided some basic guidance for developing citizen interest and organization. Although a price was charged for multiple orders, the company ran through 30,000 copies in a few months. It should also be observed that the Sears Foundation provides several graduate fellowships in planning, since one difficulty in urban renewal is the lack of an adequate supply of qualified planners.

Sears took a clear position of attempting to promote the public interest because it was in its own interest to do so. Sears' objectivity and lack of any special axe to grind is illustrated by the equal success of its handbooks among business executives, labor leaders, members of civic organizations, minority groups, or users for educational purposes. Especially telling is the nature of the membership suggested for urban renewal advisory councils in *Citizens in Urban Renewal*. The groups that should be represented run the gamut of interests, including labor, civic, religious, and minority. It is clear that Sears' concern is to find solutions to our pressing urban problems. It has not been bogged down by attachment to vague abstractions about free enterprise, the evil of subsidies, or the excessive power of organized labor.

Sears also publishes an *Urban Renewal Observer* which tells what Sears employees have been doing in urban renewal. Sears executives understand that the top brass read the leaflet and that their own advancement is promoted by their urban renewal activity. This top management support is essential if the company policy is to be more than a pious statement of good intentions.

The General Electric Company has also been one of the trailblazers in converting its employees to a program of social and partisan political activity. However, General Electric's policy has not been as enlightened as the Sears policy. It is true that Roy Johnson of General Electric is one of the moving spirits of ACTION (American Council to Improve Our Neighborhoods). However, the enlightened spirit of this organization seems not to have fully permeated the General Electric policy. There are two main threads of General Electric policy, one tending to confuse the other. First,

General Electric has promoted the Practical Politics Seminars. This is a wholly laudable effort to encourage General Electric employees to take a more active role in party politics. It is non-partisan. However, the concern underlying its interest in political parties is not its attachment to the proposition that healthy parties are good for the country and consequently good for General Electric. Rather, two special propositions seem to be at the heart of the interest. First, political activity by management is necessary to counter the political activity of labor. Second, the local community should have a good business climate. The result is that General Electric has adopted a policy toward labor that makes it difficult for the company to exercise general community leadership. The company also places great emphasis upon a low local tax structure as a prime element in a good business climate. Unlike Sears they have got lost in shibboleths about free enterprise. The participation of General Electric executives tends to be determined by company orthodoxy. For example, if a middle-income housing project involving a state subsidy is under discussion, the executive does not feel free to discuss the desirability of the project on its merits because company policy holds that the subsidy system is sapping the vitality of local communities and individuals and exploiting Sumner's "forgotten man." Therefore, the executive votes in terms of the approved stereotypes.

The second thread of General Electric policy is its interest in metropolitan area problems. For example, in the Syracuse area, George Haller, a vice-president of the company, responded to company policy and called for the organization of a much-needed Metropolitan Citizen's Council. Other citizens who had been working toward the formation of such a council urged Dr. Haller to take the lead. However, it soon became clear that the conditions under which General Electric would participate were determined by its anti-labor position and its narrow understanding of what constitutes a good business climate. Therefore, Dr. Haller and his associates did not press the discussions with general civic groups, but rather confined the exploration to business and industrial interests. The result was not a metropolitan citizens' council but a narrower organization called the Metropolitan Development Association, which was dedicated to the physical development of the area. Finally, an organization was formed whose interest and recommendations must necessarily be suspect both because it is dedicated to a particular set of goals which do not take account of other needs of the community, and because it is an effort to assert leadership by deliberately excluding important community groups from consideration. The exclusive nature of the result was in part determined by a reluctance to recognize labor's interest in metropolitan problems. It is at this point that its concern with other, largely national, issues handicaps the company in dealing with metropolitan area problems. To do this effectively the legitimacy of the claims of many interests must be recognized. This General Electric is unwilling to do because of the nature of its interest in practical politics.

Part of this difference in perspective is accounted for by the nature of the businesses. Sears policy is basically a customer-relations policy. Their involvement in the community can be more complete than General Electric's. The customers for a Sears store are the people in the community. General Electric is a manufacturing concern and its customers are drawn from the national market, including other industries. Its attachment to the local community is not apt to be so deep as Sears. Its local activity is a reflection of the New York office, since its real concern is with national economic, taxation, and labor-management issues rather than with the local community. General Electric's interest in metropolitan problems is strongest in the area of such service problems as water. It has been less vigorous in pursuing metropolitan solutions when such an approach would involve surrender of a competitive tax advantage. This results from the wholly understandable desire to maximize one's competitive advantage. Even so, this accounts for only part of the difference. Equally important are the traditional attitudes of the companies and the level of sophistication of the top management.

The moral of this comparison is quite clear. One of the most important elements in the capacity of the local community to attack its problems is the company policy, or lack thereof, of the various national concerns with branches in the community. One way to get more effective local action is first to make local participation a company policy and then to make that policy an enlightened expression of the company's self-interest. One may hope that the Sears pattern will emerge as the dominant mode of community involvement. At the same time we must recognize that manufacturing concerns are subject to a somewhat different pattern of competitive pressures and consequently their self-interest is not so readily harmonized with the community's interest.

POLITICAL VALUES

It often has been observed that the basic political fact about our metropolitan areas is the multiplicity of local governmental units in an area that is an economic, if not a social unit. We are reminded that there are over 1,000 governmental units in the New York Metropolitan Area and almost that many in Cook County, Illinois. The number of units is still rising rapidly, partly through the formation of new municipalities, but primarily through the formation of special districts.

The difficulty with this arrangement is apparent. It becomes almost impossible to provide either an efficient or an imaginative pattern of development. The resulting pattern consists of the decisions of individual jurisdictions struggling with some immediate problem but without reference to any conception of what is good for the whole area. A small sewage disposal district is formed without reference to the next one farther out that must be formed in a few years. A new water district is organized, but not under a general plan for the most efficient use of the water resources of the region. Since no institutions exist to express the common interests of the area, it is only the fragmented and immediately pressing issues that find expression in the specialized institutions that are there. It is comparable to the efforts of some men who tried to solve the problem of the Depression by planting a garden. This conduct was wholly rational from the point of view of the individual: it helped him meet his most pressing immediate need. A more satisfactory approach awaited a modification in the role of the national government. Then it became possible to talk of more fundamental remedies. It is only by creating institutions broad enough to plan for the whole region that we can develop effective expression of the interests of the region as a whole.

Three main factors inhibit the development of general institutions: first, the basic financial clash over sharing the burden for any common projects which may be proposed;[5] second, our historical attachment to the principle of local self-rule—we insist on local determination of issues which have broad repercussions beyond the boundaries of the deciding jurisdiction; third, the vested interest which local politicians have in the present system. These are fundamental factors which will continue as strong forces and can be overcome only by creating counterforces. Appeals to goodwill cannot take us very far.

The local community is subject to changing state and national standards of health, welfare, and decency. For example, we are rapidly coming to the conclusion that we should establish certain standards of safety, sanitation, and decency in housing. This is behind the move toward minimum housing and building codes. Therefore, many local communities will be under a constant political pressure from state or national majorities to achieve these minimums. Larger majorities will tend to impose their will on local majorities in order to elevate or protect minorities. Several critical questions are involved here. At which point do we convert a moral standard of the larger majority into a legal sanction. Priority should be given to the educational approach, which is unfortunately the hard way. If most local communities cannot be educated to accept the standard, then attempts at legal imposition are probably premature. There comes a time, which only prudence can determine, when the consensus is sufficiently general that obstinate communities must be subjected to compulsion. The other main issue in this regard is the desirability, where feasible, of preserving a substantial local role

[5] We have seldom had the detailed kind of financial studies suggested by Maxine Kurtz in "The Planning Aspects of Annexation and of Service Areas," *Urban Problems and Techniques*, ed. Perry L. Norton (Lexington, Mass.: Chandler-Davis Publishing Co., 1959). See also Werner Z. Hirsch, "Expenditure Implications of Metropolitan Growth and Consolidation," *The Review of Economics and Statistics*, August, 1959, and Cleveland Metropolitan Services Commission, *Government Costs: Questions for Community Decision* (Cleveland: Western Reserve University, 1959).

even when the general standard is imposed from above. In some instances this means providing alternative means of compliance. In other cases it may mean leaving the enforcement, or part of it, to the local community. In the final analysis the purpose of the enforcement is to achieve certain standards and gain willing public acceptance of them.

One national ideal which pervades the local climate is equality. It has been our contention that devotion to equality has been too exclusive and that we need to reinvigorate the ideal of freedom. However, our attachment to equality is one of the good things of life unless we become obsessed with it to the exclusion of liberty and fraternity. At the present time it finds its most powerful expression in racial matters. There is no doubt that our national moral system ultimately demands the end of racial segregation; it does not demand the end of socio-economic segregation which we protect under the banner of freedom, fraternity, and property values Our belief is really in equality of opportunity. Socio-economic segregation merely separates the more successful from the less successful. This is after all what we mean by equality of opportunity. Everyone should have an equal chance to fail as well as to succeed. Even the failures should be protected (or at least their children should) from their own inability or improvidence by providing minimum welfare standards. The purpose of equality of opportunity is to arrange this segregation in a rational pattern. The difficulty with racial segregation, and especially educational or economic discrimination, is that it is not the result of missed opportunity but is an irrational restriction. Our belief in the dignity of man and his inherent right to a chance compels us in the long run to include everyone. If certain groups fail because they do not share implicit ideals of success or even because they have inferior ability, the resulting concentration of the failures in certain neighborhoods is not segregation in a moral sense. Equality relates to the chances, not the results.

Our whole history is the story of making opportunity more and more inclusive. We have broken down property restrictions, poll taxes, sex discrimination, economic, social, ethnic, and racial impediments. At present the ideal is focussed upon racial segregation and discrimination. Therefore, the local community must operate in the context of national attachment to this ideal. It will not be free to do as it pleases. Not only has the Supreme Court converted the national moral standard into a legal standard, but many states are also developing additional standards. One item just across the horizon is forbidding discrimination in the sale or rental of private housing by state law. There are still questions of priority in the agenda and of rate of action, but it is certain that the capacity of the local community to withstand the national ideology must progressively decline. The sensible community will attempt to accommodate itself to the facts of life in such a way as to experience a minimum of disruption. We might as well pretend that the automobile doesn't exist as deny that racial segregation is coming to an end. Moral forces, particularly when they are susceptible of being converted into economic and political forces, have a character as irresistible as technology.

The grant-in-aid system was developed largely through the push of the equalitarian ideal. The grant-in-aid, whether from the national government to the state or from the state to the local community, can be viewed as a device for taxing the wealthy districts for the benefit of the poor districts. State aid to schools is a good illustration. The state decided that certain minimum standards of education should be maintained. Since this took extra money which local communities sometimes had difficulty in raising or were reluctant to raise, the state appropriated funds to implement the ideal. Part of the aid formula was based upon the need of the community, the poor communities receiving proportionately more and the rich communities paying proportionately more of the state taxes which supported the program. The equalitarian drive will continue the subsidies in existence and almost certainly apply them to new areas such as federal aid to education.

Two other forces are becoming prominent in supporting the grant-in-aid system. One of these forces is the greater productivity of state and federal taxing powers as compared with local powers. In many places we have pushed the real estate tax close to the limit. As national income rises the income tax automatically yields more income; much less so the property tax. Consequently, the grant-in-aid system is partly a mechanism for compensating for the inadequate local revenue base.

Increased reliance on higher levels of government for the support of local expenditures also arises from the fact that local communities are in competition with each other for economic development. One of the favorable factors in securing new industry is a low tax rate. As a result, communities are often deterred from raising their service level by the argument that to do so will drive industry away to a neighboring community or state with a lower tax rate. Therefore, the competition presses in the direction of low service levels. In the years ahead the main function of the grant-in-aid will be to reduce the competition between local communities in order to free their desire to raise service levels. The more local expenditures are raised through the state and national taxation systems; the more competition through self-impoverishment is muted at the local level. The more state expenditures are raised by the federal taxation system; the more subdued the economic competition between states becomes. Only by receiving large grants from central government is the local community free to increase public expenditures. The long term consequence doubtless will be ever-increasing dependence upon the federal revenue system. Attempts to push more of the revenue responsibility down to the lower levels of government will certainly fail, for these encourage a kind of competition which is destructive in nature.

The principle that we discovered with the child labor problem applies here, too. Progressive states outlawed child labor. This raised labor costs and stimulated the movement of industry to states not so squeamish about child labor. The result placed a tax upon the humanitarian impulse of the progressive state. When the economic penalties became clear, adoptions of child labor laws became very difficult to get. The only answer was federal prohibition of child labor in order to terminate a competitive situation which prevented the humanizing of our social system. Likewise dependence upon federal revenues for funds to support local services makes it possible to raise the standard of those services without driving out the very industry which helps support them.

SOCIAL FORCES

It is sometimes asserted that our central cities will soon be predominantly Negro. The Negro majority in Washington is cited as evidence. Much of this concern is based upon migration and income patterns which are projected into the future. This propensity overlooks dramatic changes that are already under way and have been for some years, as well as other changes that are just around the corner.

First, we tend to overlook the drastic changes which have occurred for the Negro since the beginning of World War II. A principle of acceleration is operating here, in which a gain in one area for the Negro is translated into gains in other areas and back again. For the first 75 years of emancipation the relation between the Negro's social habits, economic condition, educational level, and lack of political power combined to keep the Negro in a depressed condition.[6] This interrelation of factors, often considered a vicious circle, has an optimistic side. Any significant breakthrough in one of the factors is capable of being translated into the others; thus, a spiral of progress commences. Such a movement has now been under way for some years.

Without disparaging the essential early work of Booker T. Washington who tried to raise the level of the Negro's social habits, or the Rosenwald Foundation and the General Education Board of the Rockefeller Foundation which did enormous good in raising the educational level, the really dramatic changes came when the political and economic fronts were penetrated. The NAACP and a series of court decisions have been instrumental in extending the exercise of suffrage and teaching Negroes how to use their political power to promote their interests. However, probably even more im-

[6] Gunnar Myrdal, *An American Dilemma* (New York: Harper & Brothers, 1944).

portant have been the economic changes which were enormously accelerated by World War II. The United States Department of Labor estimates that the 1939 male non-white income was 41.4 per cent of that earned by the white male. By 1958 the percentage had risen to 58 per cent. The most dramatic increase was during World War II but the Negro advance has continued, although at a slower rate, since then. While this percentage is no cause for smugness it is a substantial rise in a 20-year period. In 1940 the great bulk of the Negro labor force was concentrated in unskilled and farm labor. In that year only about 20 per cent of the Negro male labor force was in the semi-skilled, skilled, and clerical category. By 1960 the percentage had doubled, so that that category accounted for 40 per cent of the Negro male labor force. They also registered a substantial increase in the professional and managerial groups. In 1940 over 40 per cent of the Negro male labor force was engaged in agriculture. In 1960 less than 15 per cent were in agriculture. In the 25-29 year age group in 1940 the white male averaged four more years of school completed than the non-white male. In 1959 the white advantage was only 1.6 years. Since 1940 per-pupil expenditures in the South for Negro pupils have increased more rapidly than those for white pupils.[7]

The implications of what is happening are quite clear. Negroes in rapidly increasing numbers are attaining the social habits, economic power, urban character, and educational level which entitle them to assimilation in the American middle class. Because of their economic and political power they will seek assimilation in places of residence, work, and education. The poverty of the Negro tended to concentrate the Negroes in the blighted areas of town. Their upward thrust will probably distribute the more successful throughout the metropolitan area. This is a counterforce to the threatened Negro domination of the central cities in our metropolitan areas.

The pattern of development of the last two decades must be modified for another reason. There are now probably less than 3 million Negroes left on farms, almost entirely in the South. The supply of Negroes to support the rural-urban migration is rapidly

[7] *The Economic Situation of Negroes in the United States*, U.S. Department of Labor Bulletin S-3 (Washington, D.C., October, 1960).

disappearing.[8] The increase in the white birth rate has partly eliminated the fear that the Negro problem will increase due to a higher birth rate. This means that our urban areas are approaching proportions of racial stability. The large influx of southern rural Negroes with little knowledge of how to live in cities will slow down. The process of education will not be overwhelmed with new arrivals. Therefore, what some people felt was an unmanageable problem is approaching a condition of relative stability. Many northern cities will still experience new arrivals, but they will increasingly come from the urban rather than the rural south. The changed migration pattern plus the rising economic level, plus a modification of social habits encouraged by the possibilities of upward mobility, plus increased political sophistication have already begun the dispersal of the urban Negro population. Soon it will encompass the whole metropolitan area.

The connection between Negroes and slums is already broken in many places. The attention of whites must be concentrated upon maintaining the character of the neighborhood, preserving socioeconomic patterns of segregation. We have a right to protect our property values, through prevention of physical decline, not of racial intermixture. The myth of mere Negro occupancy's destroying property values has already been exploded.[9] We have a modest beginning in integrated housing. There is a new breed of developer who is building subdivisions for open occupancy. Before many years most subdivisions will be open to qualified Negroes. The forces leading to residential dispersal are irresistible to the extent that the Negro raises his economic, social, and educational level because there is nothing in our political ideology to sustain resistance to the movement.[10]

[8] An excellent summary of some of the problems for urban areas arising from the heavy Negro migration to large northern cities is contained in two articles by David B. Carlson, "The New Urbanites: Nature and Dimensions," and "The New Urbanites and the City Housing Crisis," *Architectural Forum*, June and July, 1960.

[9] Luigi Laurenti, *Property Values and Race* (Berkeley: University of California Press, 1960).

[10] The sit-in demonstrations indicate that the present generation of Negroes is not willing to wait for eventual more rapid progress. Louis Lomax, "The Negro Revolt Against 'The Negro Leaders,'" *Harper's Magazine*, June 1960, pp. 41-48.

However, great problems exist for particular communities. It is probably true that exceptional progress by a community in solving the Negro housing problem, coupled with improved economic opportunity, may lead to a rapid increase in the Negro population. This is another situation in which our humanitarianism can penalize us economically. Large increases in Negro population are still undesirable in the sense that they create greater costs for services than are returned in taxes. This is a function of their low, although rising, income status. Of course, this is true only in a general way. The remedy is for the Federal government to take the lead in legislation designed to improve the condition of the Negro. This is especially true in the fields of housing and welfare legislation. To leave the matter to state or local action places a tax upon generous and humane impulses. Some communities and states will, of course, take the lead, but in self-defense they must then try to convert their own advanced standards into national standards.

In summary, we suggest that our cities should have a breathing spell in the next decade in which to assimilate the new arrivals of the Forties and Fifties. The fear of being swamped by these new arrivals should subside. For most cities the problem will probably appear more manageable in the next decade than in the last.

We are now all aware of our booming birth rate and of what this has meant for suburban development and especially for school construction needs. We are somewhat less aware of the implications of our increasing number of retired people. However, the legislative pattern of amending the Social Security Act every two years (in election years, of course) suggests a substantial degree of awareness. We can expect that the economic well-being of this group will increase faster than the rest of the population in spite of inflation. There was a time only a few short years ago when old age and destitution were synonymous for the great majority. Private pension plans, increased savings, and stock purchases or other investments have been added to the built-in political inflation of the Social Security system. The movement of the aged to warmer climates will doubtless continue. The mobility and wealth of our society will stimulate it. Fewer people have a sense of tearing up deeply planted roots, since in all probability they have moved several times during their lifetime. Often the children have already moved to another city or even across the nation. Their neighbors likewise have been constantly changing and they may already feel like strangers in a neighborhood taken over by a new batch of younger folks.

One implication of this situation is the need to experiment, in locations attractive to older folks, with new kinds of community facilities. However, there are different patterns of mobility among our population. Except for the military and some other branches of national government, mobility is greatest among the managerial class of our large corporations. Most of the professions, skilled and unskilled labor, and small businessmen have much less tendency to move (excepting some special categories of skilled labor) than the corporate managerial and engineering staffs. Consequently, in spite of our mobility, large numbers of people have attachments to their local communities. Northern cities export only a portion of their aged to the south and west. We need a much greater variety of choices for old people who desire to remain in their hometowns than now exists.

We are now only dimly aware of the implications of our tendency toward earlier marriage. Starting at about the age of 45 we will have in the next decade an enormous increase in couples whose children have married or gone to college. Many of these people will be at the height of their earning power. We have already suggested the need of experimenting with new kinds of housing and neighborhoods for them. However, what are the other consequences? Some of them we can see dimly. There is already under way a great increase in what might be called adult education. The development of arts and crafts, classes or clubs to stimulate general cultural interests, and participation in civic organizations are certainly some of the consequences. One prime consideration is the need to find better ways of utilizing the increased competence of our women. An improved audience for cultural events, new kinds of recreational and social facilities, education, business, and civic affairs are all discernible in vague outline.

We have not yet adequately accommodated our culture to the rapidly changing role of women. We still focus on an indiscriminate equality for women long after their militancy has subsided. Perhaps having granted the basic equality by and large, we can now discuss the difference without being prejudiced. The fact is that the primary role for most women is to get married and have children. Women now accept this with less resentment than in the Twenties and Thirties. However, they properly demand a broader role on the social stage. Earlier this seemed to mean the right to compete on terms of equality with men. For some women, particularly single, widowed or divorced women, this is still important. However, for most, the pattern must differ dramatically from that of the male. A common routine is work from about 18 to 24, then motherhood and home for the next 10 years or so, then back to work between 35 and 40 when the youngest child is in school full time. Thus, the life career of most women is strikingly different from that of most men. We should give much greater attention to this difference. In general our educational system gives too little attention to training women for the role of motherhood. Becoming a mother requires little training since nature has already conspired to produce that event, but raising children to live in our complex world is hardly an occupation which is completely natural. There is certainly a common core of liberal education which is necessary for both men and women. Yet when career training begins we should accept the fact that the first job for most women will last only a few years and that it is not a process of beginning a steady climb up a vocational ladder. Likewise, our educational system needs to take greater account of the needs of women who re-enter the labor force at 35 to 40. For women who are starting or returning to teaching we have already begun an accommodation. Even here, though, we tend to assume that there are no differences between the 40-year-old student and the 20-year-old. We usually give them identical courses.

We must also recognize the special problems of women in the work world. One reason that many a woman at the age of 35 considers teaching is that the hours tend to correspond to the school hours of her own children. Consequently she can normally expect to be home when they are home. Perhaps the present agitation to extend the school year will create more opportunities for work, although it cannot eliminate the need. Other vocational choices need to be adapted to the fact that working mothers have a second career at home.

Since most women work because they think the family needs the income, our rising standard of living may result in the withdrawal of some married women from the labor market. More married women work when the income of the husband is under $4,000 per year than if it is above. We should not be very sanguine about this, however, since *need* is probably more a psychological than physical term. As income rises the conception of what is required will also rise.

We require more part-time careers for women. There is no reason why industry and offices cannot begin to create special work schedules, and perhaps promotional ladders, for women. Having made considerable progress in their demand of equal pay for equal work, we should begin adapting our economic life to the special requirements of women. Some industries have already instituted, in times of labor shortage, half-shifts for college students who need the income to stay in school. This development should not be tied to unskilled and routine work only. We must realize that some women are highly talented and well-trained (or capable of being such) and that there is no special reason for restricting all of the challenging tasks to the full-time labor force. The suggestion for providing special training for women in their late thirties and early forties becomes relevant when we create new categories of opportunity.[11] Perhaps our drive to reduce the work-week should not be a uniform movement for all workers. There is good reason for giving priority to working wives. Again the principle is to provide freedom and choice. This is possible within the uniformities required by automation and mass production. Indeed, they make the process easier.

Civic affairs, long dominated by men, will certainly receive increasing attention from married women who do not choose to work. Such women have long been active in cultural affairs. Their im-

[11] A provocative proposal suggesting that women be subject to conscription for work as nurses and in other appropriate occupations which are understaffed is advanced by Marion K. Sanders, "A Proposition for Women," *Harper's Magazine*, September, 1960, pp. 41-48.

portance in politics becomes more manifest every year. With the development of organizations concerned with metropolitan-area problems, urban renewal, neighborhood action groups, and housing problems, new areas of activity open up. Increased educational attainment by women and their awareness of the potentialities of the urban environment create the opportunity for a civic role beyond anything yet known. There is much interest in these problems now on the part of women, but the conservatism of the male world still restricts their role. When the civic process is democratized the greatest influx of workers will probably come from these married women whose children have reached at least school age. They are an enormous resource. Their capacity to reach for the common good and transcend particular interests is often greater than that of their male counterparts who are more deeply involved with particular interests and, therefore, have greater difficulty in identifying with the common good.

4

The Intermingling of Public and Private

An analysis of the changing relations between the public and the private spheres of action which characterize our society can be applied with equal force to the problems of our urban areas. In general this movement can be seen as a pattern: arising in the use of regulation to prevent certain abuses, progressing to inducements to achieve minimum standards, and finally culminating in a kind of public-private partnership in order to get the most out of the system. The change in the relationship between the public and the private spheres is primarily the result of progressing from a negative concern about evils to a positive concern for potentialities.

DEVELOPMENT OF GOVERMENTAL REGULATION

In the early days of planning we were concerned with protecting the enjoyment of private property from the anti-social use of neighboring parcels. The limits to the rights of private property were generally recognized in our society. With the adoption of zoning ordinances we said, in effect, that it is legitimate for the city to restrict property rights of some for the purpose of protecting the rights of others. This is the moral limit we place on all freedom. We say freedom becomes license when it is used to limit the freedom of others or to injure the common good. However, our focus was upon the individual parcel, so that the property rights and freedom we protected were related to the parcels. Therefore, by establishing through zoning ordinances

61

certain categories and rules relating to land use we attempted to make secure a range of rights within the general framework. Planning also dealt with the provision of streets, sewers, water, schools, parks, playgrounds, and other public facilities which were necessary or desirable for the neighborhood.[1]

We accepted planning of public facilities because there was a clear understanding of their public nature. Indeed our planning of these facilities was often superior to our present efforts. But in the private sphere it was only after anguished consideration of the value of the private property system that we accepted a set of negative controls designed to prevent adverse uses of it. In general our early zoning ordinances were adopted for areas already partly built up and intended to protect those structures already in existence from encroachment by incompatible uses. In this situation planning meant the provision of public services when private decisions had created the need for them, plus a zoning ordinance to regulate the introduction of anti-social private behavior. However, the great bulk of decisions which determined the urban environment were private and only the worst of these were prohibited. Indeed, zoning was used to protect the first set of private decisions from a potentially destructive second set.

Our attachment to the free enterprise and private property system means that many of the critical decisions will continue to be private. We are not yet ready to put individuals in a straitjacket and tell them in detail how they must use their property. Nonetheless the present problem of planning is to find ways of channeling the private decisions so that the freedom of individuals is actually increased. This involves a recognition that free choice on the part of the individual relates not merely to the private parcel to which he has title, but that he also ought to be able to choose neighborhoods and even whole cities or metropolitan areas. The demand is not exclusively for control over one's individual parcel, but rather over one's environment. We have property rights in the community as well as in the parcel. There has been some shift in public sentiment to permit further controls on private

[1] A brief history of planning is contained in Ladislas Segoe, *Local Planning Administration* (Chicago: International City Managers Association, 1941).

property in order to protect public health and safety. Building and sanitation codes are primarily based upon the same premises as those that apply to zoning. Because of health hazards and fire dangers to adjacent properties we regulate plumbing and construction materials. We want to prevent epidemics and conflagrations. However, our ideological justification for them has become a little more complicated. We began to worry not only about the rights of others, but also about protecting people (or their children) from themselves, or the landlord, or poverty.

The New Deal was the flowering of a phase in our ideological development which was already well rooted. In general we can say that the emphasis on the importance of the rights of private property underwent a shift in the direction of equality. Consequently, our concern was not so much with the rights of private property as with setting a minimum level of human decency as a matter of social policy. As usual in our pragmatic culture, our first attempts were to promote equality with a minimum disturbance of property rights. The minimum standard for the urban poor was to be provided by public housing. We did not move immediately to disturb the property rights of the slum landlords by new systems of regulation, although a few cities were experimenting in this direction. We did, however, use the ancient right of eminent domain to take their property at fair value. Part of the emphasis upon public housing was certainly the result of the federal system which made this approach more appropriate for the federal government. The enforcement of stricter codes was a local responsibility.

Our national value system has moved us to promote standards of minimum welfare, old age sustenance, minimum utility service (in the Rural Electrification Administration), agricultural support, and urban housing. Since the end of World War II, it has been clear that the standard embodied in public housing has had little effect on the private market. It has also been clear that the American people were not enthusiastic about accommodating the whole lower-income market through public housing. Consequently, policy has moved in the direction of using federal subsidies for the elimination of substandard housing, but also of increasing dependence upon private industry for new housing. We have reluctantly conceded that some public housing is still necessary.[2] Steps have been taken to encourage middle-income housing under private ownership. More significantly though, we are moving to tighten public control over the existing supply of private housing. The federal urban renewal program requires an adequate system of local codes. While the federal statute does not specify a housing code regulating the use and occupancy of existing structures, nonetheless the federal administration is quietly urging the adoption of a housing code. New York State, for example, has developed a state housing code which is available for local adoption. The federal administration urges local communities in New York State to adopt the state code.

The force behind a housing code is only secondarily the desire to protect the public health and safety, although this may be the legal basis used; the code is primarily geared to guarantee a minimum standard of housing to all of our population. The hope of achieving this goal lies in a combination of public housing, middle-income private housing governmentally encouraged, and adequate codes adequately enforced. Therefore, the principle of control over private property now includes both preventing damage to other property owners and to the public generally, as well as the social policy of creating minimum housing standards. The Housing Act has decent housing for all of our population as its declared goal. Private decisions are free within the framework of the zoning ordinance which protects other property owners, the building and sanitation codes which protect the public health and safety, and the housing code which establishes a minimum standard for all housing.

Our ideals have shifted. We are not as doctrinaire about private property rights as we once were. We have given greater attention to creating a minimum standard of social amenities for all our people. This is basically due to the thrust of equalitarianism. Much remains to be done in this area. We are still creating slums faster

[2] A thoughtful review of the twenty-five years of federal activity in this field was given by Charles Abrams in an address to the Governor's Conference on Housing in Los Angeles on June 13, 1960.

than we are eliminating them. Our cities have just begun to adopt housing codes. Only a very few cities effectively enforce them. Sometimes this is because there is still a shortage of housing in the cities and too drastic enforcement would aggravate the shortage.[3] Therefore, in many communities, the critical question is how the supply of low-income and middle-income housing can be increased so that the codes can be enforced against the remainder. In some states the law has been amended to provide a civil procedure, instead of reliance solely on criminal action, to enforce the codes. In some instances if the home owner does not comply the local government itself makes the improvement and creates a lien against the property.

In spite of unfinished business, our concern for minimum standards has already changed the balance between the public and the private spheres. Yet our ideals are in the process of shifting once more. We are coming to the conclusion that preventing the worst abuses of private action for the sake of protecting the public health and safety, and promoting minimum standards permits us to plan only negatively, not positively. We are still dedicated to the private property system and individual freedom of choice but we desire more control over our environment. Most of our early objectives could be achieved through governmental action alone, but the objective of making the city a place of variety and delight involves combined governmental and private action. If our objective is that variety and choice of which we spoke earlier, then our efforts to achieve it require a new kind of planning. It can best be called community planning, for its purpose is to bring public and private actions into a mutually creative relationship. We can legislate to eliminate evils and to establish minimums, but maximums in a free enterprise economy can be achieved only by the proper combination of governmental and private action. Planning can no longer be confined to the provision of community facilities, a zoning ordinance, and certain codes. The fulfillment of more creative

[3] For an excellent case study of the politics of public housing in Chicago, see Martin Meyerson and Edward Banfield, *Politics, Planning and the Public Interest* (Glencoe, Illinois: The Free Press, 1955).

possibilities requires some process by which the sum of private actions together with public action adds up to a pleasing environment.

THE NEW PRIVATE ROLE—METROPOLITAN DEVELOPMENT

We have already observed that in the next 10 or 15 years our suburban population will grow by 25 million people unless our family ideals undergo another quick revolution. This is the most important single fact confronting those who have some hope of creating a better urban environment. Considering the magnitude of the problem, we have done almost nothing to prepare for it. The typical suburban community puts its trust in a part-time planning consultant, the self-interest of the developer, an unimaginative zoning ordinance—and the foolish belief that every thing happens for the best.

Our fundamental problem is that we have an impoverished view of what the suburb means. Our objectives for it are hopelessly inadequate. People came to the suburbs after World War II because that was where housing could be built. They came to avoid the problems of the city—the poor schools, lack of open space, social and racial antagonisms, and the dirt and noise of the city's business activity. Consequently, there is a demand to preserve or create the small town atmosphere, to banish industry and commerce, and to upgrade the zoning. This is a narrow aspiration because it elevates a single aspect of the good life into a definition. It also fails to take into account the magnitude of the population wave inundating the suburb. But above all, it works against the new developments' own self-interest. The lack of planning can be very expensive. The scale of savings can be illustrated by the town of Oak Park outside Detroit, which saw the wave coming ten years ago and prepared a foresighted plan. Among other things it set aside land, at a cost of $800,000 for the new schools and other public facilities that would be required. Had the planners waited until the last minute, as is usually done, their land costs would have been ten times as great.

Perhaps Oak Park learned the lesson from the experience of Detroit, whose expressways cost about $16,000,000 a mile to build. The same expressways can be built in open country for just over $1,000,000 per mile. We are already aware of the enormous costs of the Federal inter-state highway program, especially in urban areas. We are also aware of the huge cost of urban renewal if we ever decide to do a comprehensive job. We know the great cost of land in already built-up cities for new schools, playgrounds, street widenings, and other public purposes.[4] The tragedy is that we seem to have learned little from such examples as Oak Park. Too many communities repeat the same costly mistakes over and over again.

Many people are obsessed with community taxes. Yet few of them ever consider planning the tax rate. There seems to be little realization that the residential suburb with single family homes on large lots, each containing families with several school-age children, automatically results in a high tax rate plus private expenditures unnecessary in the city. The level of frustration and anger in our suburbs is rising because the bills inherent in our suburban developments are coming due. Citizens are beginning to cast about for remedies. A favorite one is to transfer more of the cost of services to the state or federal government. This does not reduce the over-all inefficiency or cost of the system but it does make it possible for the local community to escape at least a part of the cost of its own improvidence. So the suburbs join the cities and the farmer in the quest for state or federal dollars. While the cities get urban renewal from the federal government, the suburbs want help in handling their sewage problems.

Many developers have become concerned with the wasteful and unplanned pattern of development. Land costs are rising, site development costs continue upward, taxes rise faster than income, and the developer finds it increasingly difficult to make a profit.

The story of Jefferson Valley in Westchester County points out

[4] For an excellent summary of the legal devices for preserving open space as well as a brief account of contemporary proposals to achieve this end, see Shirley Adelson Siegel, *The Law of Open Space* (New York: Regional Plan Association, 1960).

68   INTERMINGLING OF PUBLIC AND PRIVATE

the advantages of cooperation between public and private interests in planning the development of the suburb.[5] About 1950 the Town of Yorktown in which the hamlet of Jefferson Valley is located began to feel the outward push of the suburban development around New York City. It hired a planning consultant who drew up a master plan for the Town of Yorktown based almost exclusively upon residential use of the half-acre variety. In 1957 David Bogdanoff, a Westchester County developer, acquired 670 acres in Jefferson Valley. In August of 1957 he advised the Town that the Jefferson Valley Corporation intended to develop the tract. Further he announced a plan to build at the Corporation's expense two sewage treatment plants so located that they would assist in the development of about 3,000 acres of undeveloped land. The developer then warned the town that the consequence would be a rapid development of the area with the resultant burden on community facilities including schools. He suggested that the Town restudy its determination to become a medium density residence for other economic centers. He suggested, first, that a detailed plan be made for the development of the total area in order to prevent the costly pattern of spotty development so common today; second, that the land use be planned to provide economic balance and a better tax base; third, a land-use map be developed which would locate the non-residential areas well in advance of actual development; and fourth, that the location of residential and non-residential uses be frozen, but that the usual zoning ladder be discarded. The emphasis was upon the economic and aesthetic pattern. The developer said that the Town should do the planning but that he would pay for it. The Town accepted the proposal and a very superior plan was developed. For once a town looked in advance at the relationship between its land-use plan and the community tax structure. By planning an economic balance the Town in effect planned its tax rate.

For our purposes, an interesting aspect of this story is that the developer understood that it was in his interest as well as the

[5] David Bogdanoff, "A Cooperative Approach to an Area's Future," *Planning, 1959* (Chicago: American Society of Planning Officials).

town's to plan the development. From Jefferson Valley's point of view the plan became urgent when the developer arrived on the scene. Without the frank disclosure of his intentions the Town of Yorktown would have been caught unaware. This pattern of community-developer cooperation is almost unique, but then so is such an intelligent look at the future. It is the cooperation between government, planning, and private enterprise which made the experience possible and instructive.

Another kind of public-private integration has already started to occur. We have commented on the larger scale of operation which is coming to characterize the building industry. The end result is the assumption of public responsibility, at least in the initial stages, by the private developer. Since World War II we have had such developments as Park Forest (south of Chicago) and Levittown. The private builder plans the total town in advance. The location of the houses, apartments, and shopping and community facilities is privately determined. Recently, Moss & Moss of Sacramento announced plans for El Dorado Hills, a complete new community on Folsom Lake, east of Sacramento. They already have 8,000 acres and expect to increase their holdings to 10,000 acres. The plans include homes, a central business district, a golf course, a medical center, a motel, two regional shopping centers, 11 neighborhood shopping markets, a park, a high school, three junior high schools, 15 elementary schools, a civic center, a hospital, and 10 church sites. The ultimate population of the town is to be almost 60,000 people. The developer is planning police and fire protection, Class A streets, storm drains, sanitary sewers, water supply, and sidewalks.

An even more striking example is the building of Port Charlotte on the west coast of Florida by the Mackle-General Development Corporation interests. One developer acquired 92,000 acres, 148 square miles, and has begun to build a whole new city. It has more land area than the city of Detroit. Again the developer has planned everything, even laying gas mains in anticipation of the arrival of natural gas which is still some years away. This community started out as a haven for retired people but its good planning attracted other elements, including industry. It may become a reasonably well balanced community. In addition to the facilities one would normally expect, Port Charlotte has a beach, marina, and fishing dock.

Robert Dowling's plan for Sterling Forest near fashionable Tuxedo, New York promises to create one of the most exciting new towns. It contains 23,000 acres located 40 miles from Wall Street. Dowling has planned 15,000 homes and attractively landscaped laboratories and production facilities with low nuisance ratings. This development is based upon the interesting experiment of retaining title to the land in the Sterling Forest Corporation. Residential and industrial tenants will own their buildings but not the land. This will be leased. Also their plans are subject to the approval of the developer. This is perhaps the most complete contemporary American attempt to create a planned environment for a whole town.[6]

In the twilight of his career Henry Kaiser has decided to build a new city in Hawaii which ought to become the second largest city in the state. Hawaii Kai would be built for an ultimate population of 100,000 people and involve an investment of $400,000,000. His city will include a number of complete communities, a series of shopping centers, model schools, parks, playgrounds, a marina, resort hotels, and much more.

Another interesting recent development was the formation by 880 land speculators in Florida of a single large land-owning company. They no longer compete with each other. Builders now must come to them for land. In attempting to maximize their own profits, they also have an opportunity to contribute to a more rational pattern of development.

The advantage of the kind of development represented by El Dorado Hills, Hawaii Kai, Port Charlotte and Sterling Forest springs from the single ownership of the land. The developer attempts to maximize the potential of the whole holding. In the normal situation with fragmented holdings each developer tries to maximize the return from his small holding without any more reference to the common good than is forced upon him by eco-

[6] Russell Bourne, "Bob Dowling's Woodland Adventure," *Architectural Forum,* March, 1960, pp. 109 ff.

nomics or the law. A total plan is possible in Port Charlotte without the unhappy compromises that come from competing real estate interests. If the developers are intelligent they will plan well. Such developments provide an opportunity to build an entirely modern environment. Inherited mistakes are not limiting factors. Such developments can have the same advantage that a new steel plant has over an old one. If proper attention is given to the amenities of life and the intangibles which make for greatness a standard may be set which it would be very difficult for our older cities to reach. The modern corporation may replace the king as the builder of planned cities.

The New Process Gear episode in Syracuse tells a different, but equally important, story of the relations between public and private action. In the fall of 1959 the Chrysler Corporation had pretty well decided to close its New Process Gear Plant in Syracuse and move to Auburn, about 30 miles away. They had made the decision to leave because they could not remove the obstacles to a new location in the Syracuse area and because nearby Auburn had offered cooperation and convenience as well as a free site. The newly formed Metropolitan Development Association of Syracuse and Onondaga County became aware of the gravity of losing a plant employing about 2,000 men. This was an association largely composed of business and industrial leaders dedicated to the physical development of the community. Kenneth Bartlett, a vice-president of Syracuse University and the President of the Metropolitan Development Association, and several other members of the Association flew to Detroit to get Chrysler to reconsider. Upon his return to Syracuse that night Mr. Bartlett received a call from Chrysler saying that they were sending in a negotiating team the next day. All the next day a series of meetings took place in one of the city's large law offices. Several meetings were going on simultaneously; Mr. Bartlett and State Senator John Hughes moved from room to room breaking log jams. Town, county, city, state, and water authority officials were called upon to provide satisfactory answers in their areas of responsibility. The problems of water supply, sewerage, taxes, assessments, town planning, access, and others, were hammered out. In addition, the real estate firm holding the land agreed to reduce its price. All the necessary public commitments were secured. Chrysler was satisfied that the business and industrial leadership of the community stood behind them: from Chrysler's point of view, a critical factor. They decided to build their new plant to the north of Syracuse. Through Bartlett and Senator Hughes, the business and industrial leadership had brought the fragmented political structure together long enough to resolve a problem important to the community's future. Business and industrial leadership needs to take a continuing role in planning the development of the metropolitan community, not just a temporary, last-minute one. Chaos is not a good environment in which to do business. It certainly does not attract new industry.

Our economy is expanding with great rapidity. Innovation deriving from increased research budgets means that capital investments are amortized more rapidly than ever before. Our concern for the rate of growth of the national economy means that national policy will attempt to stimulate an even more rapid replacement of old facilities. The rate at which new products are being introduced and old ones becoming obsolete is acclerating. As a result, no city can feel secure in its industrial base. In replacing old plants and building new ones to manufacture new products, industry has a broader choice of location than ever before. The inter-state highway program and truck transport is even freeing many industries from the railroad. The consequence is a spirited competitive struggle between communities for new capital investment. Existing business has a vital stake in maintaining the tax base of the community. Those depending on the local market need new industry for their own expansion. Unions have an interest in protecting the jobs of their members. Therefore, communities need an active business, industrial, and union leadership which knows how to make the complicated political machinery work to promote economic growth and development. This is a critical element in the competitive struggle between cities. Degeneration can start quickly and once under way tends to feed on itself. Accelerating obsolescence applies to cities as well as appliances.

The future will place an even greater premium upon good planning than did the past. Increasingly, good planning means the creation of environments that attract positively. Such environments must be the result of combined public and private action. Private interests must find new ways of cooperating both with the public sphere and with each other if they are to compete with the large new developments which are planned from the beginning. Metropolitan areas which are dominated by collections of small public and private interests, each pursuing its own limited goals, have about the same chance of surviving as does the corner grocer. Those industries and businesses which devote time and energy to research and planning have the best chance of survival; so do the metropolitan areas which do likewise.

THE NEW PRIVATE ROLE— THE CENTRAL CITY

If possible, the role of private planning is even clearer in the problems of revitalizing our central cities. The gradual recognition of the private role is the story of the evolution of the Housing Act. We started with public housing in the 1930's. Our objective, without being well thought through, was to eliminate slums and provide good housing for that third of the nation that was ill-housed as President Roosevelt told us. Our means were inadequate to either end as we have already commented. Consequently, in 1949 the Housing Act was amended to provide for urban redevelopment, that is, the use of public funds to clear sites for resale to private developers. This brought the private developer into the planning operation. However, slum clearance was slow and did not prevent new neighborhoods from sliding downhill so the act was amended again in 1954 to provide for urban renewal. The goals of rehabilitation and conservation were added to the program. This required active participation in planning by private citizens in the neighborhood.[7]

One of the advantages of the slum clearance portion of the

[7] A most thoughtful study of our housing programs and policies was prepared by Ernest M. Fisher for U.S. Housing Administrator Norman Mason, *A Study of Housing Programs and Policies* (Washington, D.C.: Housing and Home Finance Agency, January, 1960).

urban renewal program is that it usually eliminates the small parcels of individual owners. Relatively large urban tracts are assembled under public authority and sold to the private developer. Within the controls established by the city the private developer is free to plan a much larger area than is usually the case within the city. Close collaboration, often made difficult by state law, is essential between the developer and the local public agency. It is necessary to strike a balance between the open space, esthetics, density, and other concerns of the public planner and the concern of the private developer who desires to put the land to its highest and best use. To the private planner this usually means maximizing the economic return. The public agency must remain flexible in its planning, for events change and requests for modification of the plan by the private developer are not always dictated by avarice. In addition, it is sometimes true that the developer motivated by market considerations will suggest a worthwhile but unorthodox pattern of land use. The public planner needs to be sensitive to these market demands and guard against the tendency to think there is only one way. Yet he still must insist that the particular plan make sense in the total development of the city. For example, permitting greater densities on one parcel may not be desirable if as a collateral effect community facilities in the area are overburdened.

In urban renewal new patterns of public and private cooperation are arising. Brookline, Massachusetts, for instance, held a design competition in awarding the renewal land to a private developer. Under these conditions our theory of competitive bidding can and must be modified. The competition becomes aesthetic as well as economic. In many respects this approach, where it is practical, may be superior to a detailed list of controls established by the local public agency. Where developers are willing perhaps it would be better to give them a copy of the community's general plan including the land-use map and let the developers use their imagination in promoting the objectives established by the plan. The community could accept the best solution and then construct the appropriate zoning ordinance and other controls. Many of these developers have highly competent staffs. There is little point, except for the legal requirements under which agencies operate, in assuming in advance that their motives are bad, as long as the community reserves the final decision to itself. It might even be in the public interest to provide a partial subsidy for the preparation of the alternate designs, giving most consideration to the more successful competitors. Best results are obtained with a redevelopment project when there is a partnership between the public planner and redeveloper.

Of course, the public interest must be protected from the wrong kind of partnership. We must find ways of preventing the corruption possible in the urban renewal program, without preventing desirable innovation. The basic difficulty is that we are relying on a system of controls developed to achieve minimums and to protect one property owner from another in a situation where our concern should be for maximums. The need to protect adjacent property owners has an entirely different dimension when we are dealing with large parcels. An active public interest, plus full disclosure, may do more than rigid rules. We have a comparable problem with the civil service. It is possible to so limit the discretion of supervisors in order to prevent favoritism that the system becomes hopelessly inefficient.

Conservation and rehabilitation provide the greatest challenge to the partnership theory. Governmental power can be used to crack down on certain kinds of violations, but it cannot by itself create the individual pride and energy which is necessary in order to achieve the goals of the program. In many respects our urban renewal outlook has had the wrong focus. We assumed that it was good policy to start with the clearance of the worst areas. This policy proceeded partly from a mistaken humanitarianism, but also in part from our lack of experience in neighborhood rehabilitation and conservation. Clearance could be accomplished with a minimum dependence upon the citizenry. Government action plus the private self-interest of redevelopers could carry the load. Rehabilitation and conservation, on the other hand, require citizen organization and participation on a scale unknown in our cities. The economic advantages of conservation efforts point strongly in their favor. Most cities have many more dwelling units in danger of becoming substandard than actually existing slum dwellings. A dollar spent on conservation should save several slum clearance dollars later on. It is more important to concentrate on stopping the spread of slums than to eliminate what we have. Of course, both are necessary, but when resources are limited it would seem wiser to give more attention to prevention than we have been doing.

Detroit, for example, has probably made more progress on conservation planning than any other large city. It is estimated that the Mack-Concord project for renewing about 3,000 old houses will cost the Federal government about $2,600,000. It is reasonably sure that if the city waited until the area became a hopeless slum $10,000,000 to $15,000,000 or more of Federal money would be needed for a slum clearance project to remove the houses. Detroit has hired several social scientists to help organize the neighborhood clubs and associations to help make conservation work.

The city must help in creating the citizen organization, then it must encourage those citizens to take an active part in the actual planning of the project. The purpose of the neighborhood associations is not to provide a vehicle for carrying out a program designed by the omniscient planner. The problem is that the planner does not know enough by himself to do the planning in this kind of project. The goals and objectives must be determined by the people themselves. The planner has some useful knowledge concerning the means. He can even point out other ends that have been overlooked, but in the end the people of the neighborhood determine their goals. The process will work if the people have confidence that the city administration will follow through on its part of the bargain by providing community facilities, better housekeeping practices, code enforcement, and so on.

These vast areas of our cities threatened with decline require a new kind of planning—a harmonizing of the techniques of the professional planner, the understanding and dedication of public officials ranging all the way from the department of public works to the police, the desire of private citizens to improve their environment, and an adequate means of expressing and making that desire effective. This is another example of the change in perspective which is necessary when we switch from violations and minimums to finding ways of realizing our aspirations for a really superior environment. This objective is beyond the scope of public or private action alone.

A number of cities came to understand the need for a public-private partnership when they took a hard look at the problem of their downtown areas. Cooperation is somewhat easier to achieve here because downtown businessmen are relatively few in number and already organized. Attempts to rebuild downtown cannot depend upon the urban renewal program although some opportunities exist in this direction (as Baltimore and New Haven have demonstrated). Baltimore, Rochester, Newark, and other cities have undertaken programs to inject new life into the central core. These are cooperative ventures between the city administration and downtown business interests. Many cities have cooperated with the merchants in providing parking; many are experimenting with downtown malls. In this respect, Kalamazoo is particularly interesting. Perhaps as many as 100 cities are considering such projects. For these projects to be successful there must be a meshing of public and private activity. At long last we seem to be asking ourselves how the downtown area as a whole can be interesting, exciting, convenient, clean, and pleasant. Both public and private facilities must be upgraded in conformance with a set of objectives agreed upon by the public authority and the private interests. If these two are intelligent they will attempt to discover what their customers and citizens desire. We must be cautious about grandiose schemes conceived by hired architects or planners, especially if they look magnificent in the model. It is necessary to keep the habits and desires of the users continually in mind. The planner must find out what they dislike, what they miss, what irritates them, why they often go to the shopping center, and what would be attractive to them. It is fine to create a magnet but to do so intelligently we must know whom we want to attract and what will really attract them. Advertising has developed many excellent techniques of market analysis. Considering the whole downtown area as a product which people buy, the planner should do market research on alternate solutions to the downtown problem. We can best begin to get these answers when we have a variety of solutions to the problem. Above all beware of any single proposed panacea, like the plaza concept. It might even be desirable to bring the consumers of the urban core together with the planners as the Housing and Home Finance Agency did several years ago for the housing industry.

THE CASE OF ZONING

The changing relation between the public and the private spheres is well illustrated by our effort to modify the concept of zoning to fit new objectives. Nowhere is more hard thinking necessary if we are to emphasize the potentialities of the urban environment. Our early zoning attempts proceeded from a few observations that critics made about the unplanned city. We observed, for example, that mixed patterns of land use often had undesirable consequences. The factory blighted the store or office; the stores and taverns blighted the adjacent residences; and often the apartment destroyed the environmental amenities of the single-family house. We observed that without any control the owner of one parcel could cut off part of the light and air of his neighbor, or that an irregular pattern of set-back from the street tended to blight the neighborhood.

Zoning ordinances have been concerned with the pattern of mixed land use. The assumption is that the mixture creates blight and deteriorates property values. One of the criteria used by cities for determining the existence of slum areas is the mixed pattern of land use. The principle of zoning according to land use is now almost universally accepted, although some predominantly rural areas on the outer reaches of our metropolitan areas still resist the first attempts at zoning on the principle that a man should be able to use his property as he sees fit. Usually, shanties, trailers, junkyards, and other questionable elements have to develop to a certain point before the wisdom of zoning is accepted.

This system of zoning by use works quite well in preventing urban blight from developing. Unfortunately, it tends to force city growth into a strait-jacket. It prevents experimentation and variety. Our new subdivisions, for instance, applied the lesson too strictly. This resulted in monotonous acre after acre of single-family houses free of the supposed blight of two-family dwellings, multiple residences, stores, offices, factories, and even parks and playgrounds. The emerging emphasis upon developing positive urban values requires a new approach to the zoning problem. The old concepts express too limited a goal for our cities. We have upgraded our objectives and consequently must find new concepts for expressing them in the zoning ordinance. We know, and have really always known, that mixed land use is not in itself bad, although certain kinds of mixtures may be. We accepted the concept because it has a crude kind of justice in it and provides a standard which is easily understood and enforced. We knew that in some areas a cluster of well-maintained shops in the midst of a residential neighborhood added to the convenience of the residents, improved the character of the neighborhood, and did not destroy property values. A store owner in a residential area who requests permission to expand his parking facilities may find his residential neighbors objecting at the public hearing, not because they abstractly object to the store but because he has poor housekeeping habits in and around the store. We accepted zoning by use not because the mixture was always harmful, but because in doing so we got rid of the establishments that were most apt to generate too much traffic, block the sidewalks with deliveries, encourage rats, litter the sidewalks, serve as magnets for loafers or idle teen-agers, or create too much noise.

Rather than attempt the difficult task of finding moderate ways of controlling the evil consequences of mixed land use, it seems much simpler to prevent it altogether. In doing so we pay a price. We have made it difficult to walk to the store, barbershop, or tavern. The separation between residence and place of work has been increased. Things may be quieter, but to many they seem duller. The only casual meeting places that existed in many neighborhoods have been eliminated. This is especially important in a cold climate, because even sidewalk meetings are inhibited during the cold weather.

The mixture of land use often results from the changing character of the neighborhood. It is often true that new undesirable factors in an old neighborhood accelerate the decline. Zoning tends to freeze the pattern; it does not take into account that the city and the neighborhood are dynamic organisms. They are no sooner built than they begin to change. Our zoning concepts are static and tend to restrain the metamorphosis of areas which gives them new life. Our need is for concepts to guide the transformation from one stage of existence to another.

If our objective is to realize the potential of the urban environment and to provide a wide selection of patterns from which people may choose, then we need to find ways of reintroducing patterns of mixed land use in some neighborhoods. The question is whether a given new activity fits into the changing pattern of life. Many of the old uses that were considered blighting are now more acceptable. In addition we have learned much about performance standards. We are now better equipped to control the way in which property is used. In the early days we knew little about performance standards, so we just abolished the uses which seemed to be creating the difficulty. We now need a much more sophisticated system of zoning which is focussed, as Sergei Grimm put it, upon "levels of environment" rather than segregated uses.[8] The objective is a wide variety of patterns, gradually introduced, with consumer sovereignty ultimately dictating the distribution. There is little reason to believe that the present system represents consumer choice, since the system itself has inhibited experimentation.

Our need for zoning revision is comparable to the problem we face in building codes. In the early days, we had (and still have in large measure) specification codes which spelled out structural matters in detail. Because this inhibits technological progress, we are moving toward performance codes which protect health and safety but do not dictate exactly how these shall be achieved. However, even this conception is inadequate since the codes aim at only one level of performance. We should probably permit varying levels depending upon the circumstances. We need a comparable

[8] Sergei H. Grimm, "Some Aspects of Urban Planning," *Journal, City Planning Division, Proceedings of the American Society of Civil Engineers,* Paper 1620, April, 1958.

development in zoning. The popularity of new zones permitting offices, apartments, restaurants, and some shops suggests that our present zoning concepts have denied the consumer choices he would like to have. Our restrictions upon private property will tend to become less stringent as far as the use to which property may be put, but they will be more strict in regulating the collateral effects upon the neighborhood. If the standard is to be compatibility of new activities with the existing neighborhood, then we need to develop standards of compatibility for different kinds of situations.

Theoretically a wise man given full power could take account of all the variables in a given situation and render the best decision for that particular situation. However, our system does not accept the feasibility of Plato's philosopher king. We believe that determinate rules based upon reasonable classification are essential both to guide the discretion of the decision maker and to inform the public about our social expectations. We cannot make the law the mysterious possession of a wise priesthood of zoning administrators. Therefore, it is necessary to develop standards of felicity and compatibility so that one can generally predict what the law permits and does not permit.

We no longer need assume that single-family residences, no matter how poorly maintained, are good neighbors and that shops, no matter how well designed and maintained, are bad neighbors. The shift to standards of performance and compatibility means that governmental regulation permit new patterns, but the positive quality of the neighborhood will be determined largely by private plans. As we become more concerned with potentialities we seek ways of encouraging the imaginative citizen and property owner by revising our concept of zoning.

PUBLIC EDUCATION

Since the 1930's most of our civic attention has been directed toward great national and international problems. During the New Deal period we debated about ways of solving the unemployment problem, the role of government in economic affairs, the farm crisis, labor-management relations, and a variety of other crucial issues. With the coming of World War II we discussed the proper relation of the United States to the rest of the world, the progress of the war, how to secure peace, and all the related domestic issues. Since World War II we have been beset with the problems of the underdeveloped nations and the menace of international communism. Now our attention is shooting off into space or is at least directed toward the space race. These have not been easy times to maintain a sustained public interest in our local affairs. The mobility of our population has further reduced our capacity for local involvement. The problems themselves have become more complex. Occasionally, attention was focussed upon some particular aspect of the urban environment which had become especially irritating, but as soon as a palliative was found our attention was called elsewhere.

In the past few years there have been many signs of a renewed interest in local problems and possibilities. In the process we have come to realize that this is no casual undertaking. We are sophisticated enough to know that everything is related to everything else. As we pursue a particular concern we travel from one problem to another, from the city to the county, state, and federal governments, and from the housing development to the growth of industry and commerce. We come to understand that a wonderfully intricate fabric makes up the local community and that the knowledge required for the solution of local problems is much greater than we originally imagined.

How well is the process of public education working? In general we would have to say that this is the weakest part of the local system. In most metropolitan areas the newspapers are about the only instrument of public education of any consequence. Occasionally, the other mass media play a role but in usually sporadic and often amateurish fashion. Some organizations, such as the League of Women Voters, do a good job of educating their members. On the whole the efforts of this kind are remarkably few and usually not sustained.

Although planners have talked for many years of the importance of public education, few good examples exist. Some will remember Chicago's *Wacker Manual* which several generations of school children found exciting. We look in vain for its successors. We form World Affairs Councils in our schools to help students understand our international responsibilities, but we do not form Civic Affairs Councils to begin the education in local citizenship. The curriculum does not try to interest the student in his local community except on the most superficial level. Perhaps this is because of state control of the educational content. Often the teacher doesn't know how to relate himself to the local community. Whatever the reason there is very little real civics in which the student learns that local problems exist, that they are important, that difficult choices exist in dealing with them, that they are exciting, that there are means for dealing with them, and that he has a responsibility toward them. How many planners in recent years have made a conscious effort to interest social studies teachers in the city's problems? How many have helped prepare educational materials for instructing public school pupils? They are very few indeed.[9]

In the colleges the situation has been little better. College professors were excited by the national issues of the Thirties, by war and peace in the Forties, and by the world scene in the Fifties. Academic opportunists and college administrators let their attention be directed by the location of financial resources. There was little to nourish local government. That recently the Ford Foundation and several other foundations have become interested in the metropolitan problem is both a symptom and a cause of a reviving academic interest in the subject. It is sad to report that much of the recent concern picked up where speculation had been left in the late Twenties and early Thirties. Some of the recent metropolitan studies could have been conducted as well by the scholars of the late Twenties, so little has been learned in the meantime. Only very recently have we begun again to get deeply and intimately involved in local problems. Some hopeful signs are beginning to

[9] Reginald Isaacs in a symposium on "Public Relations and Planning," *Planning, 1959* (Chicago: American Society of Planning Officials), pp. 53 ff.

appear, but the new scholars have not yet caught up with the new reality. Perhaps in the next ten years scholars will begin to have some significant things to say about our urban environment.

Behind one of the difficulties with the planning profession, and probably government administration generally, is a switch in emphasis from public education to public relations. It is a question of how the planner views his clientele. A genuine respect for the public assumes a confidence in the public judgment once the facts are understood. Too often the planner, impressed with the mystery of his own art, seeks only consent to the immediate proposal rather than the more secure ground of public understanding. Also there is sometimes the fear that too careful scrutiny will reveal the unproved or questionable assumptions supporting the conclusion. Some planners have developed a sophomoric sophistication about having to live with political reality. As a result they play a short-sighted and amateurish political game. Some, too, are impressed with the administrative argument that they are an arm of the chief executive and conclude that their function is to implement the ignorance of the mayor, not understanding fully their obligation to educate him. Partly it is a decline in civic courage which has been almost universal. For these and many other reasons planners have generally failed in their responsibilities for public education.

Public participation in planning is not a matter of selling the plan as some administrators seem to think. This is especially true since the main purpose of planning is only secondarily to guide the physical development of the community. Primarily, it is a matter of clarifying and implementing the fiscal, economic, and social goals of the community. Even population size, particularly for our central cities whose boundaries are frozen, is a matter of social policy. Since the critical factor in planning is the set of objectives which the community has for itself, we must understand that this is beyond the scope of the planner's competence to determine. The planner has a contribution to make to this discussion because means and ends are not completely separable; however, the plan for the community must start with private interests and aspirations. A magnificent plan is possible only with an enlightened public. If the public conception of the good life is narrow and impoverished, so will be the plan. Much of the difficulty has been only the public sense of hopelessness and lack of understanding of the potential. The planner can do a great deal to arouse public interest in alternative possibilities. He can help the public understand that it is not fate that has willed the present conditions, but that they result from historical factors which were largely determined by real people making, or failing to make, real civic decisions. Therefore, the great educational function of the planner is to encourage the community to take the longer view.

It is perhaps somewhat more the task of civic leadership, including political leadership, to cure the sense of hopelessness. However, even here the first requirement is to have a set of goals which inspire. One must want to get somewhere if hope is to be restored. Then one must have a sense of power to realize the objectives. Until very recently the civic leadership necessary to the sense of capacity has been lacking. Business and industry did not think very highly of the political hierarchy. Labor leaders were concerned with the immediate needs of their members. Everyone seemed to be promoting the special interest which his occupation dictated. Few asked what was good for the community. If they did they tended to assume that promoting their own interests and perpetuating their own power was synonymous with the common good. Recently, however, many leaders of real estate, banking, merchandising, labor, industry, education, and other fields have come to see that too exclusive attention to their own interests is self-defeating. There is some real recognition now that the part will prosper only if the whole prospers. In too many communities, however, the tendency still exists for entrenched leadership to husband its power by denying the legitimacy of other claims. What they fail to realize is that if labor or minority groups are excluded they still often possess the power of veto through the political system. In some instances it will even be necessary to create the leadership for some poorly organized groups so that they can both express their own interests and become educated in the public sphere.

The defeat of metropolitan government in Nashville and Davidson County points the moral. Most of the leadership with areawide involvement, as Daniel Elazar has pointed out, favored the plan. They saw the metropolitan area as one community and generally supported the plan. However, there was another group mainly in the middle class but with a rather constricted community involvement.

> While men may work in the central city, their jobs are not the focal point of their lives; they tend to center around their neighborhood, local schools, and churches. Most of their friends and activities are confined to their own immediate areas. As a result, they really do not see the larger community as such or grasp its problems. Instead, their basic community is the neighborhood. In addition, these are people who have generally reached the limits of their upward mobility and are not primarily concerned with the growth of the metropolitan area as a means of increasing opportunity.[10]

It is here that the difficult task of public education centers. Those with a job or business involvement in the whole area are beginning to take an enlightened view of their economic or promotional self-interest. The appeal to those with a neighborhood view is more difficult to identify. In some instances their interest can be harnessed through concern for services or the tax rate. However, we must be careful about promising too much in the way of savings through greater efficiency. Many of these savings are illusory. We need a program of public education which identifies the larger community with the preservation and development of the values seen in the neighborhoods and towns. Those with a neighborhood view need to understand the dangers of unplanned growth to themselves. The newspapers have not had great success in implanting this understanding. These people tend to have confidence in their own leadership which is often involved in the broader problems. That leadership needs to be encouraged to reach out beyond the locality, in spite of the danger of repudiation if it gets too far ahead of its base.

Needed are a vision of an even better life and an emphasis upon things hoped for more than things feared. Building a solid

---

[10] Daniel Elazar, "Metro and the Voters," *Planning, 1959* (Chicago: American Society of Planning Officials), p. 73. See also James H. Norton, "Metropolitan Government: The Cleveland Defeat," *Mayor and Manager,* March, 1960.

base to move forward in a democratic society means convincing a substantial majority. We have done fairly well in terms of the community leadership in recent years; now the common man must see his interest in the whole. Perhaps the best way to achieve this is to construct our plans for the promotion of the ordinary citizen's present or potential interests rather than concentrating on the needs of business and industry. Business leadership, which has already in some instances elevated its vision one level by taking account of the needs of all business and industry, must elevate it one degree more. We need to find ways of bringing ordinary citizens into the planning process itself. There are no permanent short-cuts to the promised land. A long-term program of public education may seem too slow for many people, but in a democratic society it is the only secure basis for progress.[11]

[11] The story of one imaginative attempt at community education is contained in Eugene I. Johnson, *The Community Education Project* (San Bernardino, California: San Bernardino Valley College, 1957).

5

The Case of Urban Renewal

It is necessary to understand the complexity of the issues with which we are confronted in order to discuss intelligently our need for governmental reorganization, more effective citizen organization, and more comprehensive public education. As we have already noted, any problem eventually leads to many others in the metropolitan area. An examination of the urban renewal process, as an example, reveals the wholeness of the urban fabric. Urban renewal has the advantage of seeming, at first glance, to be confined to the particular city which has slums.[1] One would think that Syracuse, for example, could develop an intelligent program of urban renewal without much concern for the metropolitan area. In a limited sense this is true, but in a broader view even this apparently local program has major implications and complications beyond the borders of the city.

Urban renewal is the ideal case for illustrating the necessity of relating all of the plans and programs of the city to each other. There was a time, perhaps, when we could have reasonably good government in our cities if each city department did a good job in the performance of its own function. Urban renewal forces us to recognize that specialized competence is no longer enough, and that our fundamental need is to make sure that each activity is carried on with a full understanding of the total needs of the city. In a large city this is not easy to achieve. In terms of getting public facilities constructed

[1] For a good presentation of some of the policy questions involved in an urban renewal project, see Edward C. Banfield, *The Case of the Blighted City*, No. 7 in "Case-stories in American Politics" (Chicago: American Foundation for Continuing Education, 1959).

Robert Moses is a magnificent public servant. In another sense his very competence and energy is dangerous, for his capacity to get cars into New York City has outrun the capacity of the city to handle them. Consequently, his very success has exacerbated other problems. We should not put shackles on people like Moses, but we should insist that the problems arising from the energetic course of one public official shall be anticipated by the others and that the related programs be accelerated to prevent chaos. In some instances this may require temporarily restraining the empire-building administrator. Federal recognition of the vast array of factors involved in reconstructing the urban environment is most fully developed in urban renewal legislation and regulations.

A WORKABLE PROGRAM

The Housing and Home Finance Agency wisely requires that the community have a Program for Community Improvement (a Workable Program) for eliminating slums and preventing the spread of blight. This provision resulted from a growing sophistication about what is necessary in order to deal with the problem of urban blight. When communities narrow their vision to a particular project, rip out the slums, and sell the land for new development, the consequence often is an acceleration of the formation of slums in adjacent areas. Indeed this kind of approach began to look like a waste of federal money in the early Fifties. The federal government decided that it could justify the expenditure of federal funds only if the money were spent in such a way as to protect its investment rather than being spent in a way which would create the need for more federal funds.

The Workable Program requires that the community have an adequate system of codes and ordinances, an effective administrative organization for implementing urban renewal, a factual analysis of the condition of its neighborhoods as a basis for determining the treatment required, a comprehensive plan for the development of the city, a capacity to meet the financial obligations and requirements of the program, adequate organization and plans for re-housing people displaced by governmental action including urban renewal, and evidence that the program has been prepared with citizen participation and that it has citizen support.

A rigid enforcement of these provisions in the first few years would have brought urban renewal to a standstill, since hardly a community in the country met the requirements. The Urban Renewal Administration, being realistic, did not attempt to enforce the provision fully. The procedure of the URA was to require a plan for meeting the requirements. The Workable Program submissions of most communities would show that in recent years they had made headway on some of the items and promised to tackle the others. The URA would generally reply that they were happy about the progress made but would request the community to submit a timetable for compliance with the other requirements. Periodically, the community resubmits its Workable Program and the federal government checks upon the local progress. In its early days the Workable Program came to be called the "seven promises." However, as the requests for funds have exceeded the funds available in recent years the federal government has increasingly shown a disposition to call the promissory notes of the community. On the first project a community undertakes the federal government may close its eyes to the lack of an adequate comprehensive plan or citizen participation, but on the second project it is much tougher. In general, federal pressure has been used intelligently to encourage local communities to organize themselves more thoroughly and plan more comprehensively than they had previously understood was necessary.

Having decided that it wants an urban renewal program, the community discovers that as a federal requirement it must evaluate its performance in a number of areas. There are seven major steps to be considered in this process. First, the community must examine the adequacy of its regulations governing new constructions. Is there an adequate zoning ordinance? It may be discovered that variances or conditional uses over the years, plus illegal conversions, have made the ordinance obsolete. Then must begin the process of revising the ordinance, which will require a detailed land-use study. The city's planner must then try to convince the city administration and council of the need for this expensive study. The city may also decide that its zoning categories need revision and that no one on the staff is sufficiently expert to reformulate the conceptual basis of the ordinance. It may be necessary to hire an outside consultant to help with this process. The city may discover that its building code has not been modernized. This may suggest the desirability of adopting the code promulgated by the Building Officials Conference of America or the state building code if such exists. The city may be satisfied with its fire prevention code, but dissatisfied with its enforcement. The need for additional inspectors may be indicated. Probably the city has no housing code which establishes minimum standards for the occupancy of existing dwellings. Yet it becomes clear that over-occupancy is one of the basic causes of slum formation. So a housing code must be established.

The city may discover that its building, sanitary, and fire prevention codes have been enforced by different sets of officials. When they now propose to add a housing code, the question becomes one of who shall enforce it. Then in examining the enforcing process they discover, first, a low level of technical competence among their enforcing personnel which was created by either political pressure or the low salary schedule, or both. They may even discover that the administration is so lax as to suggest corruption. The city may think that, with the addition of a housing code, code enforcement should be consolidated. Why send three or four separate inspectors around to the same buildings? However, this would require a level of competence not possessed by existing personnel. Can the level be raised? Who can train the inspectors in their more complex duties? Civil service protects most of them from being fired. Even if the salaries are raised to attract more competent people most of the present personnel will remain until retirement. Raising the salary of one important group of officials results in pressures from other agencies for a general revision of the job classification system and salary schedule for the whole city.

As inadequate as the performance of the code enforcement officials has been, it may be discovered that another bottleneck exists in the corporation counsel's office. This office is usually overworked and without a lawyer experienced in code matters. It may be several months before the corporation counsel's office gets around to studying the violation reports submitted by the inspectors. Since by that time the information is out of date and cannot be used as the basis for prosecution, it is sent back to the inspector to be brought up to date. Eventually, the case goes to court. Unless a special housing court exists, which is unlikely, there probably is a backlog of housing cases resulting in a delay of several months to a year. Once again the case must be brought up to date as the trial approaches. Perhaps the city wins the case and a fine is assessed. The slum landlord may still find it cheaper to pay the fine than correct the violation. The city may decide that part of its difficulty is with the state legislation and the judicial system. Perhaps a special court should be created, a new system of fines enacted, and the state law amended to provide for civil as well as criminal action by the city. Perhaps an administrative hearing system should be instituted.

At each step there is a need for public education and understanding as well as political support. Starting out to get adequate codes enacted and enforced can stir up slum landlords, real estate people, labor unions, contractors, tax conscious citizens, as well as many others. Our purpose here is not to suggest solutions to the problems raised but to indicate the web one must unravel when starting with the strand called "codes and ordinances" of the thread called "urban renewal."

The second of the seven points calls for an adequate administrative organization. One of the most critical questions is to determine which agency will be charged with carrying out an urban renewal plan. Shall a completely separate organization be established? Shall the renewal planning function be performed by the planning commission or the urban renewal agency? Who will execute the program? Should a separate urban renewal office have its own legal counsel or depend on the corporation counsel? Should the activity of urban renewal be given to the housing agency? Since many city departments are involved in one way or another in urban renewal how can cooperation be secured? These are some of the questions that arise concerning the administration of the program itself. Often the mayor is too busy or not well enough informed to provide the required program leadership. What kind of staff does the mayor need? Should he have a chief administrative officer? Would it be desirable to appoint a development administrator to keep all city departments pulling together in revitalizing the city and to serve as the prime contact with citizen organization? [2]

Several matters of special importance need to be taken into account. The city needs to pay special attention to its organization for the relocation of people and businesses, for conducting a long term program of public education, for adopting its capital budget and coordinating the urban renewal program with other governmental programs.

The third point in the Workable Program concerns the adequacy of neighborhood analyses. The first question which this raises will perplex most cities, for neighborhood boundaries are not self-evident. Some cities may have already been divided into neighborhoods, but most will only have vague terms, such as "the east side," to refer to parts of the city.

What is generally required under "neighborhood analysis" is a study of the degree and extent of blight throughout the city. Which areas require slum clearance and redevelopment, which have some blight but can be rehabilitated without general demolition, and which have reasonably adequate housing? Much detailed information must be gathered in order to determine the answer to this question. Environmental influences of a blighting nature must be identified. Inadequate community facilities are mapped. Finally the program of treatment, neighborhood by neighborhood, must be decided on. Most important of all, the plan of action must look far enough into the future to make sure that solving the problems of one neighborhood does not create problems in another. The federal government now provides financial assistance for developing a comprehensive Community Renewal Program to make sure that each project makes its maximum contribution to the goal of total urban renewal.

The fourth point, which requires a comprehensive community plan, flows naturally from the need to relate urban renewal to other aspects of the city's development. A plan for action in the neighbor-

[2] The creation of the position of Development Administrator in New Haven is doubtless one of the reasons for the success of urban renewal in that city.

hood must be based not only on the facts in that neighborhood but upon a plan for the total community. The city is constantly dying and being reborn. When decay sets in and rebuilding is required the new land uses may be quite different from the old. We therefore need a land-use plan to guide the process of growth and renewal. That sounds simple enough, but how does the community decide what its land-use pattern should be ten, fifteen, or twenty-five years from now? The first requirement clearly is that we know how the land is being used now. This data is often lacking. Second, we need to understand how the economy of the city and area is changing. Third, we need to know which of these changes seem dictated by national forces over which the community has little control. Conversely, we need to know which are subject to local control through planning. Fourth, we require an understanding of the aspirations of the citizenry and the extent to which these aspirations are compatible with the realities. Fifth, based upon a knowledge of the present, existing trends, emerging trends, and human aspiration, the planning commission must undertake the hazardous task of projecting a desirable pattern of industrial, commercial, residential, recreational, and other developments for the future.

An integrated transportation plan for the movement of people and goods must be developed. This skeleton must be able to support the anticipated future growth. It involves considering the mass transit system, expressways, arterials, and residential streets. The plan must include air traffic, railroad facilities, and dock and port facilities where appropriate.

Such a comprehensive plan requires thinking about the future need for schools, parks, recreational areas, and other public facilities.[3] The types and location of these facilities must be determined in a general way. The difficulty of achieving this is created by such factors as automation, as it transforms our industrial life. We shall have to upgrade the technical skills of many of our workers in the years ahead. What will be our need for technical training

[3] For a particularly suggestive account of the importance of school planning, see Nathan Glazer, "The School as an Instrument in Planning," *Journal of the American Institute of Planners*, November, 1959, pp. 191 ff.

facilities twenty years from now, both for new individuals entering a labor market substantially different from the present one as well as for present members of the labor force needing to be retrained? No detailed answer can be given, but some idea of the dimensions of the problem is essential to gaining scope in our present plans for the inevitable growth and change.

The city must also have a program of public improvements which harmonizes with other programs. Street and sewer reconstruction, the rebuilding of water mains, and other improvement projects especially need correlation with the urban renewal program. Finally, plans need to be developed for each neighborhood which fit in with these over-all plans for the city as a whole. Each agency responsible for some city-wide activity needs to mesh its activity in a neighborhood with the activities of other city agencies.

The fifth point in the Workable Program requires a demonstration of the financial capacity of the city to carry out an urban renewal program. First of all, the city must know what the cost of the program will be. This is not easy to determine and involves estimates of the cost of acquiring and demolishing slum properties, the probable resale value of the land, the cost of public improvements to be made, and the increase in regular city budgets (for example, for more building inspectors) necessitated by the program. The city must then estimate what the project will do to improve the tax base of the community. Finally, it must examine the impact of the program upon the city's tax rate both in the short and the long run. If the program is well conceived it should have a salutary effect on the tax rate in the long run. However, in the first few years the city will probably have to bond to carry out the program. Can the city afford the short-term increase required or is it already pressing against some constitutional or statutory limit? Can it carry within the existing framework of state law the rather substantial short-term financing that a large urban renewal project will necessitate? What are the financial consequences of failing to undertake an urban renewal program? These are some of the financial questions the community must answer in undertaking a large program. In most of our cities, it would be a waste of money to undertake a small one.

As part of its financial plan the community should schedule its plan for public improvement and community facilities in such a way that it minimizes the local community's cash contribution to urban renewal. Once the dimensions of the financial obligation are determined and the city decides that it is within its capacity, it must decide upon the specific means of revenue to be employed.

Many communities will find the sixth point the most touchy and difficult. The Housing Act requires that people displaced by the urban renewal program be relocated in decent, safe, and sanitary dwellings at rents they can afford to pay. This requirement is difficult to meet since the vacancy ratio in most of our cities has been very low since World War II. In very few places has it risen to the normal prewar 4 to 5 per cent. In many of our cities the vacancy ratio is only about 2 per cent, or even less. This restricts the choices which people have when they choose to move. Probably 4 to 5 per cent is necessary to provide real freedom of choice for the consumer. Not only is the vacancy ratio low, but such vacancies as exist are apt to be limited in character. It may be relatively easy to get a small efficiency apartment for $90 or $100 a month but that scarcely solves the problem of the large family that can only afford $75 per month.

It is a characteristic of families requiring relocation that they often are subject to restrictions beyond the low vacancy ratio. First, many of them are relatively poor but not poor enough to qualify for public housing. Second, many of them have large families. Vacant acceptable accommodations for poor, large families are in very short supply. Third, many of them are often colored; only a portion of the limited vacancies may be available to them. Unfortunately, the pressure to get on with the program has sometimes resulted in an unsatisfactory solution to this problem. The increased pressure on the limited housing supply resulting from urban renewal or other governmental action has stimulated undesirable conversion, overcrowding, and slum development. This is especially true if the pressure is already great from an influx of new low-income groups.

In many communities plans should be changed at this point if the vacancy ratio is low, a substantial number of families are to be displaced, and a great pinch on the existing supply of lower middle-income housing exists. It may not be most important to eliminate the worst slums first.[4] The first priority may be the augmentation of the housing supply. Part of this may need to be public housing, but much of it will need to be middle-income housing. Many communities would be wise first to find one or more sites for new housing which involve a minimum of demolition and displacement of existing families. With the housing resources augmented the city is in a better position to handle the greater relocation job when the worst slum is eliminated. Indeed one can almost state as a general rule that we have concentrated on eliminating our worst slums, when we would have made better progress by increasing the housing supply first. Slum clearance is a much easier proposition if the vacancy ratio can be raised to 4 or 5 per cent, especially in the critical categories. Part of the purpose of urban renewal should be to destroy the artificial value of existing slums created by the scarcity of housing for slum residents.

The seventh point in the Workable Program is citizen participation. The federal government wisely holds that without the active support of citizen organizations urban renewal can be only skin deep. The basic citizen organizations required are an over-all citizens advisory council and associations in the neighborhoods. Many mayors need substantial urging before they will appoint a genuine citizens council. Such councils are politically unpredictable: they poke their noses into unexpected corners. Nevertheless, they are necessary in order to secure the private cooperation that urban renewal requires. Neighborhood associations are also touchy things. Any intelligent mayor knows that if he encourages their formation, the first result will be busier telephones at city hall. Complaints will increase about the bureau of building, the legal bottlenecks in prosecuting code violators, city trash pick-ups, street cleaning and snow removal, street repair, clogged catchbasins, diseased trees, recreational facilities, and many other matters. The

[4] David B. Carlson, "The New Urbanites and the Housing Crisis," *Architectural Forum*, July, 1960, pp. 118 ff.

mayor must really welcome these complaints as a means of getting a better job done if he is unwilling to stimulate citizen participation.

The implications of the seven points of the Workable Program have merely been sketched. In an actual situation they would be complicated by organizational, historic, and personality factors unique to each situation. However, this outline provides the backdrop for a successful urban renewal program.

AN URBAN RENEWAL PROJECT

So far we have discussed the complexities of setting the stage for urban renewal. Let us now consider the kinds of problems which develop in a particular project, in this case influenced by the author's experience with the Near East Side Project in Syracuse. Our objective is to discuss some of the issues that may arise in the process of developing a project. We will not spend much time on the administrative relations between the locality and the federal government. The public sees little of this and even the mayor may be unaware of most of it except when a delay occurs, a resolution of the legislative body is required, his signature is needed on a series of forms, or the federal auditor raises some question.

The early stages of an urban renewal project, especially if it is aimed at slum clearance, may proceed without much impact upon the citizenry or even on the rest of the city government. The city must first study the area and determine its boundaries, land-use characteristics, and the substandardness of the structures. This is a condition of tentatively qualifying for federal aid, and of receiving survey and planning funds from the federal government. The area is then studied intensely to demonstrate finally the eligibility of the project. After that is done the city begins to plan the acquisition of the area and its redevelopment.

In the later stages of project planning public interest begins to develop. The city must select appraisers to evaluate each piece of property. For smaller cities this may pose a problem, since there may be some question about the competence of the local appraisers. Patronage considerations may become involved. Even in larger cities it is a sensitive problem because the standards of the appraisal profession appear to be highly flexible. The city may well discover that appraisers are grouped into three classes—high appraisers, who always testify against the government; low appraisers, who usually testify for the government; and flexible appraisers, whose testimony is determined by who pays them. Compounding this situation is the legal profession's vested interest in advising its clients to permit condemnation.

In this chaotic and questionable situation the city has a very great interest in negotiating as many property sales as possible. Therefore, appraisal figures should not be so low that the angry property owner goes straight to his lawyer when he receives his offer. The appraisals should be fair and reasonable, but where there is doubt a modest generosity may be cheaper in the long run. It may turn out to be very foolish economy to select your appraisers with an eye to the lowest possible figure. In any case mistakes at this point can be very costly.

Public interest begins to be aroused when the city develops its re-use plans for the area, especially if the project is close to the central business district. This is apt to be the case with the first project, since the worst blight is usually located there. In some cases local or outside interests will begin to show interest in the property because of its potential. The city must be sensitive to these advances because they will give it a good idea of its market value. Perhaps more important will be the interest of businessmen in the central business district. They will be in favor of eliminating slums at the edge of downtown, but may worry about the establishment of competing operations and the consequent spreading out of the central business district.

In Syracuse it was decided to use the urban renewal area to build a phalanx of public and institutional buildings along the eastern edge of downtown. The purpose was both to provide the city with a civic and cultural center and to provide a governmental and institutional wall to prevent the expansion of the downtown area. The theory was that the existing downtown was large enough and should grow vertically rather than horizontally. It was also decided that the urban renewal area should provide downtown with no retail competition and with only limited office space competition. These typical decisions immediately raise a host of other questions. The plan is a good one if the revitalization of the stagnant downtown actually occurs. However, if it does not, the plan is probably ill-advised. Consequently, the appropriateness of the urban renewal plan will be determined by the vigor with which downtown is replanned and substantially rebuilt. This is more difficult than carrying out the urban renewal project itself. First, it depends much more on private action than does the project. Second, federal funds are not so available for eliminating office-building slums as for residential slums. Therefore, substantial private and local governmental funds may be required to achieve downtown revival. Third, the downtown street pattern must be replanned and thousands of new parking places provided.

Urban renewal creates the need for organizing the downtown business people for a vast project of rehabilitation and clearance. They readily understand the threat of department stores in the renewal area but do not so readily understand the need for private action on their own part. They approve of the elimination of slum residences but some of them argue against new office space because of downtown office vacancies, many of a substandard character. The city must also do a good deal of planning for downtown, preferably in cooperation with an aroused downtown group. In Syracuse when the downtown group was first organized its purposes were largely negative. Its energies were directed against urban renewal competition, zoning changes in other parts of the city which increased competition, and unfair assessments. It is the task of political leadership to convert this negative activity into a positive plan of action for the central business district.

In Syracuse the urban renewal plan pointed up the inadequacy of citizen organization and public-private cooperation in another direction. The Community Plaza which was to restrict the expansion of the central business district was to include a cultural center. Immediately, the question arises as to whether the cultural interests of the city are well enough organized to begin taking advantage of the opportunity. Again energetic leadership must help the various cultural groups to organize and learn to cooperate. In

Syracuse the cultural interests have made some progress in getting
together, but most of them are less than cordial toward the mayor.
The fine arts group has accepted a museum site in the urban renewal area, but as the urban renewal plan moved into execution
there was no real plan to implement the rest of the cultural com-
ponent. Public-private cooperation is of the essence.

The Community Plaza in Syracuse also requires cooperation between the city and the county since a joint City-County Public
Safety Building is projected. Here the minimum cooperation necessary to get joint action was secured. However, the more basic joint
planning of cooperative use of the building by the city police and
the county sheriff was slow in taking place.

Let us briefly mention the problem of cooperation between urban
renewal and the highway program. Perhaps the inter-state highway
will transform our cities as much or more than urban renewal.
Within the city it often happens that a planned highway comes
through or near a renewal area. If the city is to receive maximum
advantage from the highway it should have a well worked out
thoroughfare plan. Highway officials are under directive to take
account of local plans, but the latter are often inadequately developed. In Syracuse the North-South highway created some problems as well as opportunities for urban renewal. First, the city succeeded in getting the highway moved two blocks to the east in
order to prevent cutting the renewal area into two parts. Second,
planning on the urban renewal project was delayed because it took
so long for the state to assign the design contract—a delay caused
by a change in state administration and the peculiar politics of
awarding design contracts. From the city's point of view the
difficulty was in getting a decision on elevation versus depression
of the highway. The state spent a good deal of time studying the
possibilities of depression (which the city desired) before rejecting
it. The state, of course, had its own problems since the design
possibilities were related to the location of a connecting highway,
the route of which had not been determined at that time.

In the Near East Side Project in Syracuse a further difficulty
existed because of the low level of cooperation between the city
and the school board. It was necessary to provide some space in

the project for the expansion of the Central-Technical High School. The question concerned the amount. Realistic discussion did not begin until the Citizens' Urban Renewal Council entered upon the scene with a specific recommendation. The picture was further complicated by the unresolved question of whether development of post-high school technical training for residents of the county should be provided by the county or by the Syracuse Board of Education.

In conclusion, we should briefly mention the internal administrative problems that are involved. It is simple to say that the urban renewal program should be coordinated with the other activities of the city; as the experience of most cities demonstrates, coordination is not that easy. The difficulty lies with the lack of perspective of other department heads and with the competence of the staff available. Good planning requires more than a central agency charged with planning. It requires a research mentality in all department heads. Operating heads should as a matter of course ask themselves what the implications are for other city activities when they are considering a program. This requires more substantial knowledge of and interest in the problems and programs of the city generally than is usually found among department heads.

Part of the difficulty in many city departments is the low level of technical competence which they have at their disposal. During the Depression municipal employment could compete on very favorable terms with private employment. In many places there has been a gradual decline in quality since then. Indeed, some departments are rapidly losing their remaining competence as retirement overtakes the last of the Depression employees. When new employees are hired they may meet the minimum qualifications, but in many of the departments there are few really top notch people hired. Police, fire, engineering, public works, and recreation departments have particular difficulty. In many of these only the top two or three jobs hold any attraction as far as salary is concerned. These services are the victims of the general prosperity, full employment, and a relative drop in salary schedules. They have also been hurt by the dynamics of our equalitarian society.

Many of them used to get able young men who were too poor to go to college. Those of ability could work their way up the hierarchy. Now we have found ways of sending most of those able young men, if they have any initiative at all, to college. As college graduates they can do better in the private sector. The newer careers in planning, urban renewal, and administrative staff services are in much better shape both because of less competition from the private sector and because the salary schedules are apt to be more realistic. Even here the demand greatly exceeds the supply.

Many departments have not yet understood the importance of program planning. The consequence is that there are no long-range programs which can be coordinated. The engineering department in Syracuse has no long-range program of sewer reconstruction. Indeed they do not know the condition of the sewers in any detail. The parks and recreation department has become so accustomed to fighting to maintain existing programs that little attention has been given to new needs as the character and distribution of the city's population has changed. The assessment pattern in many cities has become an irrational hodgepodge, as much out of incompetence and small staffs as political favoritism. One can sum up all these difficulties by saying that coordinating a dynamic urban renewal program with other departments and programs is very often handicapped by the relatively low estate to which much municipal employment has fallen. Long-term effectiveness will usually require an upgrading of all municipal services. Of prime importance in upgrading these services as far as urban renewal is concerned is strengthening the planning and research function in all the municipal departments.

THE METROPOLITAN CONTEXT

Even if we master all the complexities involved in the Workable Program and in the particular project, an urban renewal program cannot be totally effective in the context of the central city alone. The city is the heart of a larger region with which it interacts. The need to put a renewal program in the metropolitan context re-

veals the inadequacy of our present governmental arrangements.[5]
In the case of any other major program we come to the same
conclusion.

If we start with the matter of land-use planning we immediately
see the difficulty. The capacity of the city to plan for industrial,
commercial, or residential development is reduced by uncertainty
concerning the plans of outlying areas. If the outlying areas may
develop a number of attractive, well-serviced industrial parks, it
is foolish for the city to try and compete in many instances. At the
time decisions in the city must be made it is often impossible to
determine what the zoning plans of surrounding towns and villages
will be. Certainly the planning of the downtown area depends upon
what the best pattern of retail trade, office space, cultural facilities,
and so forth would be for the total area. Any assumptions which
are made in planning downtown are subject to the usual im-
possibility of determining what the policy of surrounding jurisdictions will be. Similar difficulties confront us in residential development. If we accept the premise that the goal of our residential
planning should be to provide consumers with as much choice as
possible in housing and residential environment, then clearly it is
the whole metropolitan area that must supply the variety and not
any single jurisdiction. Indeed the danger in all land-use planning
is that planning solely on a local level will fail to provide opportunity and choices for certain industrial, commercial, and residential users of land. Land-use planning in an urban renewal program
is subject to all the hazards of inadequate planning on the periphery.

Similar hazards confront the planning of the circulation pattern
by the city. When the city plans its road network for the next
twenty or twenty-five years, it must guess what the suburban pattern
of development will be. An industrial concentration or a new
commercial development in an unexpected location can quickly
overload a well designed highway system. Perhaps even more basic

---

[5] For a good statement of some of the metropolitan aspects of urban renewal,
see Jefferson B. Fordham, *Urban Renewal in a Metropolitan Context*, fifth
annual Wherrett Lecture (Pittsburgh: Institute of Local Government, University of Pittsburgh, 1959).

is the problem of mass transit. Large cities, especially, may feel that it is necessary to plan the outlying development in such a way that people are encouraged to use public transportation. Greater and greater reliance on the private car may make the problems of the central city almost insoluble. Not only has the central city no control of developments in the outlying area; no one else has either. The congestion on city streets is the result of a host of diverse public and private decisions, none of which were made by people with responsibility for thinking about the whole. There must be a balance between the space allocated to the movement of people and goods and the space allocated for building. The city may decide upon the proper balance only to discover that the balance is made unworkable by the policies of other metropolitan jurisdictions.

Similar problems exist in planning water and sewage facilities. Even if the city is wise and generous enough to provide surplus capacity so that surrounding areas can hook into the city system, the city must guess where the extra capacity will be needed. Inevitably, it will often guess wrong.

The enactment and enforcing of housing codes creates another problem. Not all of the potential slum areas are in the central city. A vigorous program of enforcing a housing code may be successful in preventing overcrowding and the cutting-up of city dwelling units. However, if housing is in short supply, the pressure which the city resists by its determined effort may be transferred to the suburbs and new slums formed there. Indeed many of the subdivisions built hastily after World War II could rather quickly be converted into vast new slum areas. Some of them are already in trouble.

The problem of relocating the residents of a slum clearance area points up most directly the metropolitan character of urban renewal. When someone moves into town he customarily considers the whole metropolitan area in deciding where to live. Except for the largest metropolitan areas, it can be considered as one housing market. Therefore, problems of relocation could best be handled on a metropolitan basis. However, the local public agency can consider only the city. This is especially true in the case of plans to augment the housing supply. The city may decide that it is necessary to increase the supply of middle-income rental housing in order to make it possible to absorb those displaced from the slums. The theory might be to provide new housing not as a direct relocation resource, but as an increase in general supply. However, the city often discovers that the only open land suitable for the construction of such housing is located outside the city. Consequently it may be prevented by the limits of its jurisdiction from adopting the most sensible relocation plan.

One special aspect of this problem is the need to open up wider opportunity for minority groups displaced by governmental action. Even if the city cannot plan for them beyond the city limits, they still should have suburban housing available to them if they satisfy the economic requirements. It is contrary to the American goal of free opportunity to force colored families back into slums who have demonstrated their educational and economic capacity to leave them behind. State legislation will probably be necessary in order to hasten the removal of barriers. This movement is already under way. Relocation can be much more easily handled when minority groups are realistically able to consider the housing supply of the whole metropolitan area.

SUMMARY

We have atempted in rather broad outline to indicate the complex and inter-related issues and problems which confront a community when it decides upon an urban renewal program. Comparable complexity would have been the result if we had selected any major urban problem. Our purpose in attempting to portray the broad fabric is to point several morals. First, our elected public officials are competent or incompetent largely in terms of their capacity to master the network. Old-style efficiency and adminisstrative ability is only one of the skills they need. Above all else the modern mayor needs to be able to see the ramifications of a particular program in advance. He cannot wait until difficulties arise. He must anticipate and take them into account. That is, he must have a mentality which understands planning and research.

As our previous discussion has indicated, his concept of planning must be much broader than mere physical planning.

Second, this complicated network is the reality with which citizens organizations must deal. In important matters it is no longer possible to concern oneself with a special project or program and push ahead ignoring the rest of the social fabric. Effective citizen participation must rest upon a high degree of sophistication, which we are, perhaps, beginning to achieve. Liaison and clearance must be established with other groups working upon the same fabric but with different starting points.[6] Citizen groups are important partly because they are often less limited by jurisdictional inhibitions and divagations. The complexity of the fabric also suggests that it is vitally important for major citizen organizations to have a technical staff of their own. Maximum effectiveness will rarely be achieved without this aid, both because technical matters often become central and because citizens can rarely devote enough time to follow out all the threads.

Good citizenship requires intellectual sophistication and the mastery of this complex network. Good intentions are a starting point, but no more. The complexity which our examination of urban renewal reveals is representative, not unique. The intricacy of this fabric provides both challenge and stimulation to professional and citizen alike.

[6] Two recent publications suggest the seriousness with which many businessmen now take the need to acquire mastery of urban complexity. The Chamber of Commerce of the United States has published a *Community Development Series* (Washington, D.C.: 1960). Titles included in the series of booklets are, "Balanced Community Development," "Community Analysis—Foundation for Decision Making," "Comprehensive Planning—Guide for Community Growth and Change," "Planning Urban Renewal Projects," "Modernizing Local Government," "Financing Community Development," and "Community Leadership—Key to Local Development." The Committee for Economic Development has published a good policy statement by its Research and Policy Committee, *Guiding Metropolitan Growth* (New York, 1960).

6

Governmental Reorganization

The problem of finding more effective governmental ways of dealing with the complexity we have been discussing cannot be solved by any one general prescription.[1] Too many people have been looking for *the* solution. Too many metropolitan studies have already been conducted with the conclusions predetermined. We must look for solutions to metropolitan problems in each particular metropolitan area. Our attempts to generalize about the metropolitan problem are better directed toward mechanisms by which progress can be made rather than toward generalized solutions. Consequently, the emphasis here is upon creating bridges to the future rather than designing tables of governmental organization which could exist after twenty years of hard work. Getting an image of the future is important, but it should be a substantive image rather than one of a reorganized governmental structure. No one gets excited about an abstract governmental form. The real problem is how the forms can be made to satisfy more adequately the needs of men. Therefore, we need to create a situation where adaptation is encouraged. Given the nature of many metropolitan problems this requires action at the federal, state, and local levels. Some generalized solutions may be possible at the federal and state levels, but local solutions will be particular.

[1] A good summary statement of the problem of government in metropolitan areas is Robert C. Wood, *Metropolis Against Itself* (New York: Committee for Economic Development, 1959).

THE FEDERAL GOVERNMENT

It is not our purpose here to discuss the total impact of the federal government upon the local community or to enter the discussion of whether we should have a Department of Urban Affairs. Such structural changes too often create only illusions of change. After more than a decade of "unification" of the armed forces through the creation of the Department of Defense it may be seriously questioned whether much unification has in fact occurred. Therefore, before we talk seriously about a Department of Urban Affairs it might be helpful if we raise the question of how well the Housing and Home Finance Agency is now functioning and whether it is unified. Ernest Fisher has outlined the main problems:

> Most of the criticisms of the programs administered by the HHFA can be grouped under five topics: (1) each program concerns only a fragment of the whole housing and urban environmental problem; (2) action under the program has taken the form of isolated projects without reference to an over-all program of improvement into which the projects should be fitted; (3) the programs and the character of projects undertaken have remained similar throughout the years although profound changes have come in economic, social, and political conditions; (4) the federal agencies supervise and control local public agencies too strictly; and (5) there has not been as flexible use of and experimentation with the various programs as there should be. Too often an effort has been made to try to use the wrong means to accomplish a desired purpose.[2]

The first two points are of particular interest to us here for they suggest federal impediments to a more comprehensive approach to our urban problems. The HHFA is now a collection of autonomous units. A good deal more rationality could be injected into government in the metropolitan area by unifying that agency. As it is, the Urban Renewal Administration is dedicated to the elimination of slums, yet it often seems that the purpose of the

[2] Ernest M. Fisher, *A Study of Housing Programs and Policies*, prepared for U.S. Housing Administrator Norman P. Mason (Washington, D.C.: Housing and Home Finance Agency, January, 1960), p. 13.

Federal Housing Administration is to subsidize the creation of the slums of the future. Mr. Fisher correctly points to "projectitis" as one of the besetting sins of the present policy. Within one city there may be loan guarantees on housing developments, public housing, a college dormitory, and urban renewal. Each project is approved by a different autonomous unit. The basic difficulty with the project approach is the mental set which it gives to the local government. Therefore, Mr. Fisher proposes that all community projects be put into one consolidated grant contract. This certainly has the advantage of forcing both the local government and the federal government to look at the total package and see how the parts relate to each other. The emphasis upon the project has resulted in local communities rushing to get their share of federal funds without asking very carefully where they were leading. A consolidated grant contract is a step in the right direction, but only a step.

Mr. Fisher goes to the heart of the matter when he emphasizes the importance of developing a comprehensive long-range program. Federal subsidies for this purpose, on a dollar for dollar basis, are much more important than capital grants. In its large Near East Side project, the City of Syracuse is asking for a capital grant of approximately $11,000,000. It would be much more sensible (assuming only $11,000,000 of federal money is available) to give the city ten and a half million dollars for the project and $500,000 to develop a total program. In 1959 Congress amended the Housing Act to permit federal grants for the development of comprehensive renewal programs. In any rationing of funds the comprehensive renewal program should have priority over capital grants.

We have already commented upon the way in which the Workable Program requirement is being tightened to stimulate better planning by the individual city. The consolidation of all federal aid into one contract would permit extending the Workable Program requirement to all federal programs, especially public housing and community facilities. Such a device would encourage local planning and enforce better cooperation, or even force consolidation, at the local level. Within the limits set by local politics and personalities this kind of local consolidation is to be recommended. However, it would be a bit bizarre for the federal government to insist upon consolidation at the local level of housing, urban renewal, and perhaps planning, while continuing a series of autonomous units at the federal level.

So far we have been talking about the city which receives the federal aid. Is there anything the federal government can do to encourage a metropolitan approach to the problems of housing and urban renewal? Even here the government could begin to experiment with the Workable Program requirement on a metropolitan basis. A really adequate program must be metropolitan. Such an approach perhaps becomes more feasible as the federal program for aiding suburban communities in building sewage disposal facilities gets under way. To make a metropolitan Workable Program effective requires federal benefits that are desired by the suburbs as well as the central cities, like the loan guarantee program. Of course, urban renewal and occasionally public housing are important to some suburbs. Suppose the federal government were to make these programs, including FHA insurance, contingent upon a Workable Program in the metropolitan area. Such a program, gradually implemented, could have an enormous impact upon metropolitan governmental organization. The result would be to utilize the spirited competition between metropolitan areas as a device for achieving metropolitan planning and action in the housing and renewal fields. Federal programs are fundamental in maintaining and improving the metropolitan area's competitive position.

Our purpose here is not to spell out the details of such a federal program, but to suggest a general approach through which our national values and programs can be made effective. We should not use national power to destroy things local needlessly, but we cannot permit an outmoded localism to thwart the political, moral, and technological imperatives of the age. Therefore, the grant-in-aid system should be used to encourage an approach more in harmony with these imperatives. The requisite to a more creative use of federal power in restructuring metropolitan areas is the consolidation of various programs at the federal level, plus a federal acceptance in its own operations of the importance of that research and planning which it insists upon at the local level. Having created a system of dependence upon federal funds, the federal government can either continue to subsidize the obsolete and out-moded, or else insist upon new patterns of local action as a condition of receiving the subsidy. The imaginative and restrained use of federal power is certainly to be desired in preference to a policy of bailing out the inefficient and outmoded.[3]

THE STATE

The state is even more deeply involved in our metropolitan areas than the federal government.[4] In the fields of education, health, hospitals, stream and air pollution, road and highway construction, recreation, and other areas the state is constantly influencing the metropolitan environment. In some of these fields, such as highways and hospitals, the federal government is also involved through grant-in-aid programs. However, it is more appropriate to discuss these as matters of state government since, unlike housing and urban renewal, the federal government deals with state agencies and not directly with localities. Therefore, the problem of relating these activities to each other and to local plans and programs is a state responsibility even though federal money is involved. It may be that Congress should require a Workable

[3] The most authoritative statement of the relationship between the federal government and metropolitan areas is Robert H. Connery and Richard H. Leach, *The Federal Government and Metropolitan Areas* (Cambridge: Harvard University Press, 1960). This is one of the technical reports of the Government in Metropolitan Areas Project under the direction of Luther Gulick and supported by the Edgar Stern Family Fund. The authors do not favor a Department of Urban Affairs. They properly make the point that the problem of coordinating the activities of various federal agencies in the metropolitan area is more a matter of clarifying policy than of administrative reorganization. This requires staff work at the presidential level rather than the creation of a new department which they believe would create more problems than it solved. Nonetheless Connery and Leach do not give sufficient weight to the symbolic importance of departmental status.

[4] The Government in Metropolitan Areas Project also has a technical work in preparation under the direction of Luther Gulick and Charlton Chute on the states and the metropolitan problem. When it is published it should be the most complete statement of the issues available.

Program as a condition for receiving highway funds, but it would be a requirement put to the state rather than the locality.

Coordinating the activities of the state in a particular metropolitan area is very difficult. The heads of state departments are normally powerful individuals, often elected officers, who in any case have substantial support in the legislature. They develop their power and make their reputation by pushing their own functional programs. The competition for funds and power is one of the strongest characteristics of the bureaucratic system and it leads to secrecy, political manipulation, and poor communication between agencies.

It is doubtful that the activities of the state affecting local communities could be grouped together in one department and then subdivided on a metropolitan-area or regional basis. We tend to set minimum standards of performance by function. Our legislative committees and our interest groups are organized in that fashion. One cannot imagine the education lobby consenting to put power in the hands of a state regional administrator with authority to determine educational policy along with housing, health, highway, sanitation, and other policies. The immediate objection would be that education is too important and technical to be put in the hands of a general administrator. Other functions of government would raise a similar cry. The conclusion seems inescapable that the functional basis of state administration will continue largely intact. To create a Department of Local Affairs might help in some areas of activity, but still provide one more competitor for taking on new functions in other areas.[5] If there are a number of minor functions not intimately related to the major areas of state administration, perhaps consolidation of these activities in a Department of Local Affairs would be modest progress.

In the long run it will be more useful if an Office of Local Affairs concerns itself with research, planning, and communication rather than operating programs. In many instances this would require first that the existing departments strengthen their staff

[5] Luther Gulick has made this suggestion in "Metropolitan Organization," *The Annals of the American Academy of Political and Social Science,* November, 1957, pp. 57-65.

resources so that they can do significant research and planning. Few state departments now fully understand the importance of these staff activities. State highway departments, for example, may hire highway planners, but few of them hire economists, business experts, and political scientists to help them see more than the engineering problems of highway construction. However, under federal pressure they are just beginning to do so. Further, the department is usually so autonomous that it is unaware of such specialists in other departments. Even when aware, it seldom has the competence in its own department to use them. Therefore, the first requirement is to get the functional departments to develop a more sophisticated conception of their own programs and to understand that their actions have far-reaching effects.

With more expertly staffed departments an Office of Local Affairs could provide several useful services. First of all, it could devote itself to the problem of communication between functional areas. The Buffalo agent of such an office, for example, might preside over periodic meetings of a council of state officials for the Buffalo metropolitan area or possibly for western New York. Such councils could serve a very useful service if they had the support of the governor, his budget officer, and the legislature. The regional agent of an Office of Local Affairs could take the lead in stimulating a flow of communication between state agencies. He might take special responsibility for calling attention to considerations which are overlooked because of functional orientation.

The most useful function of such an office would probably be in the area of fact gathering and distribution. If each department became better staffed to do research related to its function, a great need would exist for coordinating the various research efforts. Even now, when much research is primitive, duplication exists. However, the Office of Local Affairs should attempt to coordinate more than the research efforts of state departments. Many local governmental agencies, private associations, and public utilities do research on the metropolitan area. The Office of Local Affairs could serve as a clearing house for all these efforts and even make suggestions to federal agencies in the area. Much of the present effort is now wasteful, since many separate agencies may make population projections, economic studies, and other such items. More important, much vital information is not gathered because the need for it is unknown. For example, if a welfare department does research on its clients it does so to satisfy its own needs. However, the housing staff may also need information on welfare clients but of a slightly different sort. If the welfare people knew the nature of the housing need when the research was being undertaken they might be able to satisfy it with very little extra effort. The Office of Local Affairs could attempt to make researchers in one division aware of the broader implications of their work and encourage them to do their research so that the decision-making process is illuminated, not only in their own department, but in others as well. The Office of Local Affairs could then become an intelligence center for the metropolitan area. Its purpose would be to mobilize all the available intelligence for officials at all levels of government and even for private groups.

The Office of Local Affairs might also staff itself with some first-rate planners. Their function would not be to plan the metropolitan area, but to question state, federal, local, and private agencies concerning planning in their area. Their function would be to act as catalyst rather than actually to plan. The research and planning staff of the Office of Local Affairs should also have authority to do research themselves in order to fill gaps. They might even do research for other public agencies on a contract basis. Many local and state agencies do not have the professional competence for research. They should be able to turn to the Office of Local Affairs to get it done. This approach could also reduce some of the adverse effects of the consultant system. It is clear that such an Office of Local Affairs would have to possess unquestioned technical competence and top-level support to fulfill the leadership role that has been projected for it.

Such an office might perform one other function of great importance. It could serve as a public information center. It ought to become expert in translating the knowledge which it has into terms understandable to the interested layman. Again the professional approach is absolutely essential to prevent the accusation of propaganda peddling. Public education as well as the education of officials is necessary to wise decision-making. Materials might even be prepared for classroom work in the public schools.

Clearly we can get a more coordinated approach to the problems of the metropolitan area if state agencies acquire the habit of discussion and consultation with local agencies. State highway engineers in many places have left a trail of ill will because of failure to consult those who had an interest in the result. Reliance solely upon a public hearing at the end of the process is scarcely adequate. If fear of speculation in land is the problem which has inhibited communication then we must find some way other than secrecy to protect the public interest.

One of the difficulties has been that local plans are not well developed. Highway engineers have been under injunction to take account of local plans, but such seldom exist outside of the central cities. As in the case of federal aid to housing and urban renewal, it would seem wise for the state to encourage or even to subsidize local planning. State highway funds might be conditioned upon a highway plan for the metropolitan area. Most county highway departments do very little planning. Gradually the requirement might be extended to cover other related planning elements. In the long run highway funds cannot be spent intelligently without a transit plan and a land-use plan. In general we can say that great progress can be achieved by distributing state grants only on condition of long-term plans for spending the money wisely. Such a prerequisite might not lead to governmental consolidation in the metropolitan area, but it should lead to greater cooperation and joint planning. This procedure has led to a great consolidation or centralization of school districts in recent years. The centralization was considered necessary to achieve a more efficient utilization of resources, raise minimum standards, and provide wider opportunity and choice for our school children. The same principle has unrealized potential in other areas.

As in the case of federal participation in metropolitan areas, one of the basic requirements in the states is a better mechanism for formulating policy. Perhaps an Office of Local Affairs could provide this over-all policy consideration in the governor's office without assuming control of program areas. The governor needs a staff agency, whatever its name, to assist him in formulating policy. The problem of advising the legislature is much more difficult. Probably legislative leaders need more staff assistance than they now have. However, some effort should be made to educate individual legislators. The best way to begin on this problem is to upgrade the competence of the staffs of legislative committees. Devices should then be developed for improving communication at the staff level. However, there is no device which can substitute for a state legislator of good quality. Greater concentration of public attention on their work would provide both a democratic check and the kind of recognition which increases the prestige of the position.

THE LESSON OF TORONTO

The act of the provincial legislature of Ontario in 1953 establishing the Municipality of Metropolitan Toronto raised hopes on the American side of the border that something might be done about reorganizing our own metropolitan areas. The critical role played by the province in achieving the federation suggests that we must be careful in drawing conclusions from this success. The principle of local home rule never developed in Canada to the same extent that it did in the United States. Consequently provincial intervention to reorganize Metropolitan Toronto did not offend Canadian sensibilities to the same extent that similar state intervention would in the United States.

Toronto had applied to the Ontario Municipal Board in 1950 for the progressive amalgamation of the thirteen municipalities in the area. The Town of Mimico had alternatively applied for the establishment of an inter-urban administrative area. In January, 1953 Lorne R. Cummings, Chairman of the Ontario Municipal Board, issued "The Cummings Report" dismissing both applications and recommending the establishment of a metropolitan municipal government. In the same year the provincial legislature passed "The Municipality of Metropolitan Toronto Act" creating a federal system of local government. The individual municipalities retain control over local matters and are directly represented in the Metropolitan Council which has authority over those matters deemed areawide in character.

The crucial element is the role of the province. The federation was created upon recommendation of the Ontario Municipal Board by the provincial legislature without requirement of local ratification.[6] It is generally agreed that had a popular majority been required in each of the 13 municipalities the federation would not have been ratified. It is doubtful that a majority of the total area could have been mustered. It is also generally agreed that if the people of the metropolitan area were asked today whether they approved of the federation it would be overwhelmingly supported. This fact has led some people to suggest the desirability of placing greater responsibility in the state for reorganizing our metropolitan areas. Such a move has much to recommend it. In Virginia there is a somewhat comparable procedure that is judicial rather than legislative.

We have a stronger tradition of home rule in the United States than does Canada. It is doubtful that many states could be brought to accept a system that did not provide for some form of local ratification. One can only hope that some state will find the courage at least to experiment with state adoption. A procedure somewhat more in keeping with our traditions would be the creation of a state agency with power to study and to recommend metropolitan reorganization in particular instances. This might be one of the duties of an Office of Local Affairs. Such a study could be initiated by application from a municipality or from the county. The objective of such a procedure would be to inject both expertness and impartiality into the recommended solution. The highest competence would be necessary to make such a process successful.

A means should be found of preventing small localized majorities from thwarting the general will of the metropolitan area. In some states traditions of home rule are so strong that the consent of each unit may still be required. The ultimate objective to be sought is a simple majority of the metropolitan area. A half-way solution would require concurrent majorities in the central city and in the

---

[6] The Greater Winnipeg Investigating Commission has proposed the creation of the Municipality of Metropolitan Winnipeg, also without a public referendum.

area outside taken as a unit. In the end the health of a democratic society must rest upon the capacity of such majorities to recognize the distinction between what is truly local and what is an areawide concern. To continue to give a veto to a majority in a small jurisdiction means minority rule if the greater majority is prevented from taking action which they deem commensurate with the problem.

The recommended approach would require constitutional revision in most of our states. We certainly should not place all our hopes on such revision, since most state legislatures over-represent rural and small-town interests. Also, suburban communities often feel a strong attachment to home rule. Consequently, the path of constitutional reform will not be easy and other solutions must also be sought. In any case, constitutional revision will be the result of continuous public education over a long period of time. We cannot expect revision unless the need for it is generally recognized.

In many states constitutional revision could well take the tack of permitting the creation of urban counties. Such a provision does not exclude the procedure already suggested. The functions of counties have been expanding. They are becoming important administrative units for a wide variety of federal grant-in-aid programs. Constitutional revision permitting the adoption of home-rule urban county charters would be in line with existing developments. Such a procedure would permit transcending small local majorities. The best provision would be to require only a simple majority of the county taken as a whole to create such a charter. The requirement in New York, for example, that a county charter must have a majority in the central city and a majority in the rest of the county taken as a unit is an obstacle, but not a complete bar, to constructive action. New York law has the further disadvantage of requiring a majority in the villages of the county taken as a unit if any transfer of function is proposed.

In most of our urban counties a prior piece of business needs attention. Before we can seriously consider the urban county we need a modern and effective administration of that unit of government. It is still largely a collection of autonomous administrative units often with the political patronage system still in control, only loosely coordinated by the Board of Supervisors. Therefore, the creation of an effective county manager, county president or other elected executive, or county president-manager system is a prior condition to the transformation of an urban county into a general governmental unit. We need to raise the reputation and competence of county government before the people will feel secure in vesting it with broader powers. This requires both an over-all executive and possibly the election of at least some members of the legislative body from a large geographic area, possibly the county at large. We will probably not make maximum progress so long as county supervisors represent towns or townships. Political statesmanship will develop when the electoral base transcends the small vested interests.[7]

Money is at the root of much of our difficulty. The competition between parts of the metropolitan area has resulted in tax inequalities. The value of property has become adjusted to the prevailing financial jumble. Consequently, it is impossible to revamp the financial base of support within the metropolitan area thoroughly without creating new injustices. To raise taxes substantially in a tax haven is to reduce the market value of the property and work injustice against recent purchasers who paid a price which capitalized the old inequity. A fair solution will probably require a gradual shifting of the tax burden from the property tax to sales or payroll taxes. The objective should be gradually to shift the financial support of governmental services to a metropolitan tax base in order to reduce over a period of time the relative importance of the existing inequalities. In this way we can gradually reduce the political importance of the present inequalities. To attack them directly is to invite failure.

For most of our smaller metropolitan areas the goal of county reorganization would seem to be an adequate solution and a natural development of our historic institutions and values. In all

---

[7] While I firmly believe this generalization is a good general rule it should be observed that the experience of Metropolitan Toronto in which the councilmen represent the old units suggests that such locally based representatives can develop a metropolitan mentality.

likelihood the transformation of the county will be a gradual process and take many forms. Therefore, we should not spend too much time trying to decide what the final outline will look like, but rather know in general where we are going and take one step at a time. First, improve the administrative machinery of the existing county; second, transfer welfare, or some other function, to the county; third, create a county planning body; fourth, transfer another function—public health, for example—to the county; and so on piece by piece. One must always remember that it is necessary for a consensus to be developed supporting a broader basis of operation. Often this agreement comes function by function. It is probably true that general schemes of reorganization will be both necessary and possible when a particular metropolitan area lets things get so bad that a general revolution becomes feasible.

THE METROPOLITAN COMMUNITY

The example of Toronto both presents the best case for metropolitan government in existence on the North American continent and indicates what we mean by metropolitan as distinct from local concerns. Grodzins and Banfield take too narrow a view when they say:

> When the needed distinction is made between "problems which exist in metropolitan areas" and "problems which exist by virtue of the inadequacies of governmental structure in metropolitan areas," the latter are relatively few. Transportation is probably the most common and most pressing of the real metropolitan-area problems. Other common and important problems are air-pollution control and civil defense, and in some areas, water supply and waste disposal. Opinion rather than technical considerations may add other functions to the list.[8]

An examination of the functions of the Municipality of Metropolitan Toronto indicates that they have gone somewhat beyond

[8] Morton Grodzins and Edward Banfield, *Government and Housing in Metropolitan Areas* (New York: McGraw-Hill Book Company, Inc., 1958), p. 156.

the minimum list of Grodzins and Banfield. The Metropolitan Corporation is responsible for the following services:

1. The uniform assessment of all industrial, commercial, and residential land and buildings.
2. The construction and maintenance of a water system for wholesale distribution to the municipalities.
3. The construction and maintenance of trunk sewer mains and treatment plants which accept sewage from the municipalities on a wholesale basis.
4. The enforcement of air pollution control regulations.
5. The designation and establishment of an arterial system of highways.
6. The provision of a public transportation system for the metropolitan area. The Toronto Transit Commission has a monopoly of, and is responsible for, public transportation.
7. Certain planning and financial responsibilities in the field of education, in cooperation with the Metropolitan School Board. This Board does not manage or administer schools. Financial support is substantially metropolitanized.
8. The hospitalization of indigent patients, post-sanatorium care for consumptives, provision of homes for the aged, and the maintenance of wards of children's aid societies.
9. The provision and maintenance of a Court House and jail.
10. The provision of public housing and low rental housing for the aged. This is not an exclusive power since the City of Toronto also builds public housing.
11. The exercise of jurisdiction over practically all aspects of licensing.
12. The provision of a unified police force.
13. The preparation of an official plan for the metropolitan area and all adjoining townships including land uses, ways of communication, sanitation, green belts and park areas, and public transportation.
14. The establishment of metropolitan parks.
15. The organization, administration, and operation of all civil defense services.

16. The levy of a metropolitan tax to support its operations and the handling of the capital requirements of local municipalities which no longer issue bonds.

Technical considerations, rather than mere opinion, argue for the metropolitanization of most of these functions[9]—not that metropolitan government is the only way they can be performed: even the Grodzins-Banfield list can be performed without it. The fact is that technical considerations cannot be divorced from other considerations. Few will question that the metropolitanization of the assessment procedure would result both in a more competent job and consequently in a more just distribution of common burdens. The state equalization process has eliminated only the gross inequities. Few will deny that in most metropolitan areas the metropolitanization of the crime laboratory, communication system, and record-keeping system would result in more competent police work and perhaps greater efficiency. The fact that poor elderly people tend to congregate in the central city because of public housing, public transportation, greater access to social agencies, and other reasons may not require metropolitan support of the indigent aged, but the fair distribution of the burden is technically very difficult without it. Grodzins and Banfield argue that communities should be permitted to maintain a low level of services if they so desire. If this means that welfare clients, indigent aged, the indigent sick, the bright schoolchild, low-income groups in need of public housing, town residents in search of recreation, and other groups for whom no services, or inadequate services, are provided must look to the central city for services, then it does not follow that the suburbs can escape these burdens by claiming they are too small to supply them or that they do not want any residents who require them. A community can maintain a type of control which makes it impossible for any poor people to live in the community, but if it does so it must bear its share of the burden by allocating

[9] For a summary of progress in Metropolitan Toronto, see Frederick G. Gardiner, "The Face of the City Has Changed," Metropolitan Council, 1960. Since Mr. Gardiner is chairman of the Metropolitan Council his report is not dispassionate, although it is accurate.

these functions to a government with power to tax the rich and the poor community alike for the support of the necessary services.

The fundamental objection to denying the metropolitan character of many of these activities lies much deeper. Grodzins and Banfield seem to assume that government is defined by the services it performs and that, therefore, the scope of what is necessarily metropolitan is defined by the technical requirements of performing the service. As a result, they leave planning out of their list of necessary functions. It has been the heart of our contention that the problem of government is to encourage the creation of a variety of facilities and environments so that the individual has a wide range of choice at each stage of the life cycle. To achieve this we must have an intimate meshing of the public and the private spheres. It is the task of governmental planning to help create the choices and to guide the public-private interaction. Any individual community in the metropolitan area is technically incapable of providing the range of choice required. Therefore, if a range of alternatives is considered desirable, metropolitan planning is necessary.

The experience of Toronto is instructive. The metropolitan government permitted a bold attack upon the highway and mass transit problems, the development of adequate water resources, an end to waste disposal chaos, a better meeting of school needs, the unblocking of the recreational impasse, a more just distribution of tax burdens, the beginning of a more adequate housing program for low-income groups and the elderly, better policing in many areas, and other achievements. The consensus is that while the residents of the area did not know in advance that they wanted these things, they now consider them progress and would think themselves deprived of a great blessing if they were removed. The argument that people like things the way they are is not an argument against metropolitan government but for public education.

The tendency in Toronto will doubtless be in the direction of greater amalgamation rather than less. That course will be supported by public opinion. The example of Toronto gives us a goal to shoot for in our governmental reorganizations. Generally we will proceed step by step rather than all at once, but the movement will not stop with the meager list supplied by Grodzins and Banfield. They have understood neither the purpose of government in our time nor the relation of one service to another. To suggest that solving the housing problem has little to do with the metropolitan area indicates a lack of understanding of the actual problems with which housing and urban renewal officials must contend. This is especially the case in relocating and housing low-income and lower-middle income groups, the indigent or the partially incapacitated elderly, and those requiring nursing homes. To suggest that one can adequately develop a transportation system without land-use planning is to invite disappointment.

DADE COUNTY

Metropolitan Dade County represents the second instructive development on the continent. On November 6, 1956 the people of Florida passed an amendment to the state constitution permitting home rule for Dade County. The people of Dade County were overwhelmingly in favor of the amendment. In most states such a constitutional amendment permitting county home rule should be one of the first items of business. The creation of metropolitan government in the United States will generally come under the home-rule banner and not by legislative fiat as in the case of Toronto. However, the content to be poured into the "home rule" slogan should refer to the county (or other broad local jurisdiction) and not the town, village, or small sewer district.

On May 21, 1957 the people of Dade County adopted the proposed charter by a scant 51 per cent of the votes cast. There were several reasons for the low margin. First, any particular application of the principle of home rule is certain to have less support than the principle itself. Second, the charter board made few political compromises but concentrated upon getting a charter as close to the ideal as possible. Third, the defense of the charter was left to second-line, though devoted, people. Fourth, most of the existing political organizations combined to defeat it. With these handicaps it must be accounted a great triumph that the charter passed at all. The basic principle of the charter will doubtless be imitated in other places. It did not try to achieve city-county consolidation as had an earlier proposal in 1953 which was only narrowly defeated. The existing municipalities maintain their identity and under the provisions of the charter cannot be abolished for local purposes without their own consent. This was a wise concession to local feeling, since it does not obstruct the capacity of the county to act on metropolitan matters.

O. W. Campbell, the first county manager, has summarized the basic responsibilities of Metropolitan Dade County:

1. To streamline the internal functions of the county government into an efficient team working together for the common welfare of all the people.
2. To provide a governmental organization capable of dealing with area-wide problems.
3. To provide tangible benefits to all communities within the metropolitan area in the form of improved services, more comprehensive services, a more equitable distribution of the tax burden, and a means of solving problems that individual municipalities are unable to solve for themselves because of limited municipal charter authority.
4. To provide a framework within which the advantages of having separate community political structures may be retained.
5. To resolve the problem of over-lapping, or competing authority and responsibility between central government and the municipalities.[10]

The charter recognized the basic importance of reorganizing the existing county government. However, the charter was attacked before this task could be undertaken. The opponents of the charter organized and submitted an autonomy amendment which would have protected the existing powers of Miami and the other municipalities and ended the hope of real metropolitan government. Fortunately, the courts delayed the election on the amendment scheduled for February, 1958 to September, 1958. In the inter-

---

[10] O. W. Campbell, *The First Annual Report on the Progress of Metropolitan Dade County, Florida*, p. 4.

vening seven months the new metropolitan government began the massive task of overhauling the county government. By the time the election was held the county government had been completely revamped. Particular progress was made in modernizing budgetary, financial control, and personnel matters. Several new programs were developed. The number of departments was reduced from 35 to 17. Before the election a substantial tax cut was announced. On September 30, 1958 the autonomy amendment was defeated when 59 per cent of the people registered their confidence in the new government.

Metropolitan Dade County is still not a metropolitan government in the sense that Toronto is. This is not important, for the government is still young. The main point is that its home rule has two important facets. First, it is free from the interference of the state legislature which can no longer pass statutes for Dade County alone. Second, the people of the county have the power to decide their own destiny by simple majority vote on a countywide basis. These conditions of progress metropolitanize nothing themselves. The county government has a charter for attacking metropolitan problems on an areawide basis. Metropolitanization will occur slowly or rapidly depending upon public opinion and the record of performance of the government. The actual development of metropolitan government will doubtless occur step by step. The new government was especially wise in establishing a generous planning budget.

Even the relatively modest progress which Dade County has achieved will be difficult to imitate elsewhere. A peculiar set of circumstances made the prospects especially favorable. Harry T. Toulmin, the former Director of the Budget in Dade County, answered the question of why the voter was "pro-Metro" this way:

I think the answer can be found in a combination of circumstances: explosive growth, the ineptitude of traditional governments, a population consisting largely of displaced persons, the people's lack of respect for local officials, their distaste of state domination in local affairs, power of the daily press in moulding public opinion, stupidity of anti-Metro tactics, development of an excellent and saleable plan for governmental reform, and superior administrative leadership in the months preceding the critical autonomy election.[11]

The first three factors particularly distinguish Dade County. Population increased by 85 per cent from 1950 to 1959. This is nearly the most rapid rate of growth in the United States. When this fact was combined with the special ineptitude of government in Dade County things reached crisis proportions not often duplicated. Few other communities would have allowed such a backlog of problems to accumulate. The displaced character of the population served to increase the power of the press because of the consequent weakness of local social organization. Nonetheless this explains only why Dade County was first to break new ground. If their experiment is successful, as appears likely, other communities may be induced to undertake similar action before things reach crisis proportions. It is part of the peculiar logic of events that a great new step forward should be taken by one of our governmentally most backward communities. A corollary probably is that those communities which successfully ameliorate their worst problems will in all likelihood be the last to get really modern governmental machinery. Perhaps more intensive efforts at public education can induce change at a lower level of discomfort. Certainly an understanding of the potentialities may do so.

INTER-COUNTY SUPERVISORS COMMITTEE

A third kind of governmental approach is represented by the Inter-County Supervisors Committee in the Detroit Metropolitan Area.[12] When Edward Connor became President of the Wayne County Board of Supervisors he initiated discussions of common problems with the presidents of other boards in the metropolitan area. Thus the Inter-County Supervisors Committee was born. Citizens may find it hard to believe that practically no channel of

[11] Harry T. Toulmin, "Metro and the Voters," *Planning 1959* (Chicago: American Society of Planning Officials), p. 64.

[12] Edward Connor, "Before trying metropolitan supergovernments . . . first make intelligent use of the governmental machinery already existing," *The American City*, July, 1959.

communication had previously existed. Wayne County had not been in the habit of consulting with Oakland or Macomb counties about common metropolitan problems. Even informal communication was really non-existent. Now there is a regular vehicle for the exchange of views and the formulation of common policy. For maximum effectiveness it will be desirable to transform urban counties into governments of general jurisdiction.

In other instances chief administrative officers in a metropolitan area have begun the creation of a similar device. For example, we now have a New York Metropolitan Council. At lower levels there are a few examples of technical collaboration, such as the code enforcement program in the Detroit Metropolitan Area.

The improvement of channels of communication and consultation is one of the basic considerations in approaching our metropolitan problems. The premature attempt to solve such problems with some massive governmental reorganization only makes enemies out of those who are potentially allies. The approach typified by the Inter-County Supervisors Committee is particularly important in our larger metropolitan area. Detroit's metropolitan area now includes six counties; in a few years it will be ten counties. The development of more viable political institutions for dealing with such vast urban areas will be a matter of political evolution. No one can now say what forms will finally emerge. No one seriously advocates permitting matters to degenerate into a crisis of such severe proportions that some bold new scheme may command popular support. The only alternative is to begin building bridges to the future. The Inter-County Supervisors Committee is exciting because it is one such bridge.

Both legislative and administrative bridges have to be constructed. Bridges with and between state agencies, with special purpose districts, with school districts, between a variety of technical people including planners, between private groups such as chambers of commerce, manufacturers associations, labor unions, and civic organizations, and between one chamber of commerce and another all must be constructed. They have the first priority and the advantage of developing public understanding and agreement. Our type of democracy does not permit an easy way out. We value the autonomy of local units and private groups and the separation of the legislative and the executive functions. These values can continue to have vital meaning only if links are created between the units, groups, and functions. Without linking we will find it almost impossible to reinterpret the meaning of these values creatively, in the light of technical, economic, and political change. Where public understanding is sufficiently developed to permit governmental reorganization it should, of course, be pushed, since a metropolitan government can best create the needed images of the future. These plans in turn further promote public understanding and even more imaginative action. The difficulty is that community understanding and efforts at metropolitan action must be substantially developed before a popular base exists to support governmental reorganization.

The construction of a great variety of bridges and links provides a basis for moving ahead. This does not contradict our earlier assertion that we need a sense of the possibilities of the future. The point, rather, is that governmental reorganization will often come at the end of the process, not at the beginning. The creation of bridges is vital to the development of the dreams, which in turn is the condition of governmental reorganization. The Inter-County Supervisors Committee is an institution in which men can think and plan in terms of the possibilities of the whole region. Without such institutions thought is forced back into an archaic pattern. In the beginning it is not necessary that such bodies have any legal basis or authority. It is important, however, that the constituent members have authority to act upon their part of any plan or project. This differentiates the Inter-County Supervisors Committee from earlier regional planning associations.

7

Citizen Action

The decade of the 1950's saw the rapid growth of citizen interest, organization, and action on the urban scene. This citizen action was stimulated on the one hand by the decay of our central cities and on the other by the problems of metropolitan growth. Citizen action concerning the problems of our older cities began slowly as the decade opened, was greatly stimulated by the citizen participation requirement of the Housing Act of 1954 and by the organization of ACTION (American Council to Improve Our Neighborhoods) in the same year, and was torrential as the decade closed.[1]

Citizen organization and action arose from three main causes, in addition to concern over urban problems. First, the ideas, institutions, and tools with which most city administrations attempted to meet the problems of decay, blight, congestion, racial relations, and so forth were antiquated. Citizen action was usually necessary to stimulate public officials, to develop modern building and housing codes (and especially to insure their adequate enforcement), and to get city planning taken seriously. Second, urban renewal required private action if it was to be successful. Stopping the spread of blight is simply beyond the capacity of the city government without private assistance. In addition city administrations were slow indeed (and still are) to understand the nature of the task. There is a bright spot here and there, but our mayors' understanding of the dimensions of their

[1] ACTION, Inc., 2 West 46th Street, New York 36, N.Y., has been of great help to local groups ranging all the way from neighborhood associations to metropolitan citizens' councils.

duties and of the means of performing them is still rather limited. Private action and public education are the essential pre-conditions of more sophistication in city hall. Third, the existing governmental jurisdictions and ways of transacting business were not commensurate with the dimensions of our metropolitan problems arising from rapid population growth and the attendant urban sprawl. Citizen organizations and action moved into this governmental void.

In a general way citizen action and understanding started with the neighborhood. However, as our comprehension of the problem matured we saw the necessity of action on a broader and broader scale. By now, the metropolitan approach is generally considered necessary. There has also been a growing understanding of the role of state and national policies. In the field of race relations, at least, consideration of our international reputation has been relevant. The early neighborhood councils have not been abandoned. Their importance is no less now than ten years ago. However, we now understand much better the limits of neighborhood action and the importance of citywide policy, a metropolitan approach, and a reorientation of state or national policy. To get an understanding of the very great variety of citizen organizations now involved in our local governmental problems let us look at some of the specific types. We shall not discuss new roles for older organizations such as chambers of commerce or social agencies.

NEIGHBORHOOD REHABILITATION

If this new type of citizen organization can be said to have any particular beginning, it was probably with the formation of the Hyde Park-Kenwood Community Conference at the end of 1949. This neighborhood which includes the University of Chicago was perhaps the first one in our country which tried to come to grips with the twin problems of urban decay in a middle class neighborhood and large scale Negro immigration. It was an effort to reverse the processes of decay and create a stable interracial neighborhood. The four working committees were responsible for block organization, community planning, community survey, and community organizations. It should be observed that this neighborhood was especially rich in leadership potential. The well-known names of Harvey Perloff, Martin Meyerson, William Bradbury, Maynard Krueger, Herbert Thelen, Robert Merriam, Reginald Isaacs, St. Clair Drake, Everett Hughes, Philip Hauser, Lawrence Kimpton, and Julian Levi are among those we find associated with the conference in one way or another. The community also had excellent church leaders and many others, perhaps less well known nationally, of high competence.

It is not our purpose to retell the story of the Hyde Park-Kenwood Community Conference; Julia Abrahamson has done that with passion and excitement in *A Neighborhood Finds Itself.*[2] Rather, we want to emphasize the importance of such an organization in dealing with a major racial problem, getting people to care for their property, providing tot lots and recreation areas, getting the streets cleaned, putting incessant pressure upon public officials to enforce the codes, getting businesses and restaurants to adopt an interracial policy, stopping the spread of panic over the racial issue, upgrading the public schools, and encouraging the city to take urban renewal action in the neighborhood. These and many other things can be done (or at least begun) by a neighborhood council. However, even this list makes it clear that some matters of citywide concern are involved. Early in the story it became evident that Hyde Park-Kenwood was an inadequate planning unit and that the citywide supply of housing was a major concern of the neighborhood, since the housing shortage, particularly for Negroes, was the dynamic force behind illegal conversions and overcrowding.

In spite of very great activity in recent years in the formation of neighborhood councils, perhaps the main advantage has derived from their inadequacy. The story of ACTION is particularly instructive on this point. In the beginning it was oriented toward a "fixup, paint up, patch up" kind of campaign to inhibit the spread of blight and decay. Gradually the inadequacy of the neighborhood approach became apparent. One of the early difficulties

---

[2] Julia Abrahamson, *A Neighborhood Finds Itself* (New York: Harper & Brothers, 1959).

where large-scale clearance was involved was to interest capital in redevelopment projects. Because of its broadly based membership ACTION was instrumental in carrying the message to financial interests. Of course, the federal and local authorities also helped. Mainly it was the attitude of hope for our central cities which ACTION and the Urban Renewal Program helped create that led to increasing interest on the part of private redevelopers. In recent years private capital has developed a lively interest in urban renewal. The shortage of capital, as far as clearance and redevelopment is concerned, has been largely eliminated. The question of interest rates is now the main uncertainty.

The problem of financing the rehabilitation of declining areas has not been fully solved, mainly because our planning concepts have not been adequate to the task. Perhaps it would be better to say that cities are only now going ahead with active clearance and seriously studying rehabilitation. James Rouse, ACTION's president, was one of the founders of the Fight Blight Fund in Baltimore which is designed to finance rehabilitation. However, this example has not been generally imitated.

CITYWIDE ORGANIZATIONS

The Cleveland Development Foundation took a somewhat different tack. The basic problem in Cleveland was the housing shortage. In these circumstances it became clear that large-scale clearance would place an intolerable burden on the housing supply. In all likelihood relocation of people from clearance areas would be impossible or would result in further overcrowding of an already inadequate housing supply, thus accelerating the formation of new slums. Therefore, a basic requirement was to increase the housing supply. Since it was organized in 1954 the Cleveland Development Foundation has invested 2.3 million dollars in increasing the supply of housing, particularly for lower-middle income groups. More than 5,000 units have been completed or are under construction. The number of available rentals has substantially increased, thus making clearance of blighted areas possible without overcrowding new ones. In most of our cities the vacancy ratio is so low that the development of relocation housing should precede large-scale clearance. Since private developers have become interested in relocation housing in the last few years, it is less of a problem now than when the Cleveland Development Foundation was formed. The present difficulty is more often lack of an adequate site for construction, particularly since the city can act only within its own boundaries.

The Oakland Renewal Foundation has acted mainly as an educational force in the Clinton Park project, Oakland's 78-block area rehabilitation project. It is now possible to get conventional financing in the area. The Buffalo Redevelopment Foundation's efforts have also been largely educational but on a very broad base. It has been a kind of gadfly, information center, and community coordinator. The Citizens Redevelopment Corporation in Detroit, supported by all the major interests in the community, got urban renewal going when the Gratiot project threatened to bog down permanently. There are other examples of citizen action to promote urban renewal on a city-wide basis. Their purposes vary depending upon the locality, including financing rehabilitation or relocation housing, education, and the support of research studies. ACTION's James Rouse is also a member of Baltimore Neighborhoods, Inc., which is interested in creating stability in neighborhoods that are in racial transition. While much of the concern of the groups mentioned above may be concentrated in a particular renewal area, they are also citywide groups dedicated to the renewal of the city, with a citywide perspective. The development of these groups indicated that while the neighborhood approach was essential, it was inadequate by itself.

Perhaps one of the major contributions of ACTION was that it brought a wide variety of interests together, including business, industrial, real estate, building, labor, civic, religious, and minority groups. As a consequence many national organizations now have a policy of promoting urban renewal. This is very helpful on the local scene, since the local individual is supported by his national affiliation. It is also possible to secure participation because of the prestige of national backing. Perhaps most important is the example of national cooperation between various groups which helps to generate the same kind of local cooperation.

CENTRAL BUSINESS DISTRICT

It was natural for businessmen to be particularly concerned with the deterioration of the downtown areas. They have an enormous investment in the central business district which is threatened by traffic congestion, deterioration, lack of parking, and competition from shopping centers and new office areas. The general concern over urban renewal plus such successful achievements as Pittsburgh's Golden Triangle has sparked a hopeful new vitality in downtown business people. The January, 1960 issue of the *Journal of Housing* was devoted to "The Businessman's Role in Renewal." The following sample of article titles gives a faint idea of what is going on as far as downtown is concerned:

New York: "Wall Street" to be Redeveloped: Rockefeller Leads Way
Spokane: Businessmen raise $150,000 for Center-city Study
Washington: Downtown Businessmen Out to Renew Center City
Boston: Chamber of Commerce Backs Renewal
St. Louis: Downtown Brought out of Doldrums by Businessmen
Milwaukee: Nineteen Milwaukee Businessmen Unite for Center City Renewal
Kansas City, Missouri: $15 Million City Center Renewal Sparked by Businessmen
Baltimore: Businessmen Undertake Nonassisted Downtown Project

These are only some of the cities which have programs for the revival of downtown. Almost every city of any consequence is developing a scheme for downtown revitalization.

Baltimore's Charles Center project, particularly, has stimulated enormous interest. The clearance of a 22 acre site downtown is involved. The rebuilding, estimated to cost 127 million dollars, will start soon. It is noteworthy for several reasons. First, great attention has been given to aesthetic considerations and open space, as well as to underground parking and new commercial facilities.

Second, the Greater Baltimore Committee, a group of businessmen, is responsible for the project, which was originally scheduled to be financed by private and city funds alone. It was later decided to seek urban renewal assistance. The city's investment was expected to come back to it in increased tax revenues in less than 20 years, even before urban renewal assistance was sought. Now the city's investment should be returned much sooner. The revitalization of downtown is only one concern of the Greater Baltimore Committee, which realizes the necessity of attacking the whole range of metropolitan problems.

The importance of comprehensive planning for the city as a whole has received almost general acceptance, if one judges by the comments at the "ACTION Program for the American City" held in May, 1959 at Newark. James Rouse inspired the delegates by declaring that the tools had now been fashioned for a total attack upon the problems of the city. Mr. Rouse indicated that some of the tools, particularly housing codes and the power to condemn for redevelopment, had become available only very recently. It was clear at the conference that to transcend the project and think in terms of comprehensive planning was the new ideal. Citizen organizations from now on should deal with the totality.

THE METROPOLITAN APPROACH

It was also clear at the ACTION Conference that the next expansion of conception was already under way. The concept of comprehensive planning was already transcending the meaning the Federal Government had ascribed to it in the Housing Act of 1954. Increasingly, citizen organizations must raise their sights beyond the central city and think in metropolitan terms. The names of the Allegheny Conference on Community Development, the Greater Philadelphia Movement, the Greater Baltimore Committee, and the Greater Trenton Council suggest the developing perspective. It was especially interesting that Edward Banfield's doubts about the possibility of governmental reorganization of the metropolitan area were greeted at the Conference with a kind of anger. It will not do to be a man of little faith even if the obstacles are enormous.

Indeed, here is a real challenge to citizen leadership, since it is no longer a problem of pressuring existing governments, but rather one of creating new governmental institutions.

The Greater Trenton Council illustrates the fact that medium-sized as well as larger cities are adopting a metropolitan approach. The Council has a membership which is broadly representative of the metropolitan area. It is privately financed and non-partisan in its approach. The Council is also representative in that its membership is drawn from business, industry, labor, religious groups, and civic organizations. The various levels of government are also represented.

The Council came into existence, like its counterparts, because mushrooming metropolitan problems and central city deterioration were outrunning the capacity and control of the area's governments. In terms of priority the Council's first concern was the revitalization of downtown. Much of their work was necessitated by the previous lack of planning in Trenton. Consequently, it was necessary to make a study of land uses, parking, and traffic in order to formulate highway, parking, and public transportation plans. It also studied the development of a civic center, a governmental building program downtown, a recreational, cultural and historical area, and down-town urban redevelopment. The deepening of the Delaware River suggested the desirability of a study of port facilities. A metro-politan highway program was investigated with particular reference to an inner loop. Lastly, the Council decided that its long-term objective was a metropolitan area plan, although the central city problems were to receive first attention.

Hal H. Holker, the Executive Vice-President of the Greater Trenton Council, has described one of the basic advantages of such a citizen group as compared to public agencies:

> . . . a private group such as ours has a broader and more independent outlook, which frequently permits more objectivity. It is truly metro-politan in composition. Therefore the veiwpoints more accurately reflect our interest in the sound short- and long-range economic development of the total area, including the center city and the suburbs. Unfortunately, more often than not local public groups that represent political subdivisions within the metropolitan economic

and geographic area see their interests as quite different from others in the area. . . . a private group can cross political boundaries and move up and down the governmental scale much more freely than can the public agency.[3]

Perhaps the most interesting part, to date, of the Trenton effort is the development of a "General Neighborhood Urban Renewal Plan" for the whole downtown area including the blight that surrounds it. The plan covers approximately one square mile and is designed to give the region a vigorous heart.

The well-known Citizens Action Commission in New Haven has a similar orientation. Its original focus was in New Haven rather than the metropolitan area, but it, too, became concerned with the larger orientation. This group has approximately 600 people involved in its work. It is an advisory body to the mayor. The city's technical experts also have close relations with its various committees. The work of the Commission is suggested by its six main committees: the Downtown Action Committee, the Industrial and Labor Development Committee, the Neighborhood Improvement Council, the Human Values Committee, the Citizens Advisory Committee on Education, and the Metropolitan Approach Committee. The depth and breadth of citizen participation is suggested by the constituent parts of the Committee on Human Values: Dixwell Neighborhood Program Advisory Committee, Subcommittee on Health and Welfare, Subcommittee on Juvenile Delinquency, Bicycle Loan and Safety Committee, Case Interpretations Committee, Neighborhood Projects Committee, Committee to Study the Relationship between Delinquency and Work Opportunities for Adolescents, and Subcommittee on Recreation. New Haven has probably come closer to mobilizing the entire resources of the community in order to create a bright new tomorrow than any other city.

Another type of organization is represented by the Valley Development Foundation in the Binghamton, New York area including all of Broome County and the Metropolitan Development Association for the Syracuse metropolitan area. These are primarily

[3] Hal H. Holker, "The Relationship of Official and Citizen in Planning Programs," *Planning 1958*, American Society of Planning Officials, Chicago, pp. 99-100.

organizations of businessmen dedicated to the problems of both the central city and urban sprawl. In each case the focus is upon economic opportunity and development. The following purposes of the Valley Development Foundation, except for some difference in emphasis, are substantially the same as those of the Metropolitan Development Association: to supply guidance and direction and marshal support for public and private urban renewal projects; to stimulate the community's concern and interest in its orderly growth and the economic stability of the greater trading area; to supplement and assist in coordinating the work of local planning agencies; to encourage private investment. The foundation maintains liaison with local public agencies and private groups, particularly the chamber of commerce. The main virtues of such a group include the education of its own membership, the stimulation of other private groups and public agencies, probably gaining of financial support for necessary research and planning studies, and its role as a medium for expressing the interest of the business community. However, because of their unrepresentative character such groups cannot have as sharp a focus of action as the Citizens Action Commission in New Haven.

Another type of citizen organization is the regional planning association that actually engages in planning, including such examples as the Regional Plan Association of New York, the Pittsburgh Regional Planning Council, and the Planning Council of the Greater Baltimore Committee, Inc.

These metropolitan or regional planning organizations arise from the inability of our political structure to plan on a regional basis. Therefore, citizens who feel the need of an intelligent approach on a metropolitan or regional basis form an association and hire professional planners. They may work in greater or lesser degree with existing planning staffs in the area, but maximum effectiveness requires some separate staff. The main advantage of a regional planning association with powerful backing and a technical staff is the freedom and imagination with which the future of the region can be considered. Acceptance of its ideas depends upon the quality of its relationships with private enterprise and local public authorities. Such an association can often focus attention upon a particular problem, such as highways or recreation, in a way public agencies cannot. Such planning activities, despite the often unrepresentative character of the sponsoring agency, pose little danger of undemocratic results since political acceptance is necessary. However, undemocratic consequences can result if the local governments possess little planning expertness to review the proposals.

This discussion has not exhausted all the types of new citizen organization. Nor has it commented on the new perspective of many existing organizations. For example, in some cities the broad perspective of city redevelopment has been pushed by the local chamber of commerce and other existing local groups.

Probably the main impression that results from viewing this burst of activity is the prominent role which businessmen are playing. What is heartening is that many of these businessmen are developing a well-rounded sense of what is required to make the city truly attractive. As James Rouse has expressed it, "It's about time we stopped *apologizing* for beauty, feeling we always have to find some 'practical' reason or 'economic use' for doing something. To create a park because it makes a more beautiful city is reason enough. Beauty is an enormously strengthening, vital force in the city. It is a protest against disorder."[4] An editorial in the *Journal of Housing* put it in somewhat more organizational terms when it said: "So—as money begins to talk through the businessmen who are getting into the renewal field, it's important that plenty of well informed and articulate spokesmen for the public interest and for the truly humane city be on hand to raise their voices, too. What's needed when money begins to talk: a conversation; not a monologue."[5]

A MODEL

A kind of "ideal" organization emerges from the experience of recent years. However, local history and personalities will interpret

---

[4] "ACTION's Rousing Mr. Rouse," *Architectural Forum*, May, 1959, p. 129.
[5] "Money Talks," *Journal of Housing*, January, 1960, p. 3.

the "ideal" in many ways. Its outline is dictated by the experience
of many groups in recent years. Repeatedly it has been discovered
that a constructive attempt to approach any basic problem of the
metropolitan area leads from issue to issue, agency to agency,
government to government, and personality to personality. The
parts, although important, can be approached with maximum
effectiveness only in terms of the whole. Therefore, a metropolitan
citizens' council, either with official representation or close working
relations with the relevant governments, emerges as the desirable
framework. In this way the fragmentation of the formal governmental structure may be partly overcome by informal organization.
As a minimum such an organization can begin and carry on discussion in terms commensurate with the problems. It also provides
a forum for discussing really imaginative proposals for the future
of the whole area. The lack of such a forum is one of the disadvantages both of fragmented government and decentralized citizen
organization. Just as it is necessary to create an institutional framework which will encourage political leadership to think in terms
of the whole, it is equally necessary to create such a framework for
civic leadership.

A representative council would probably be a rather large policy-
making group and would require an executive committee. It would
also need the services of a professional staff. It ought to be broken
up into a number of working committees which might take some
such form as the following:

1. Urban Renewal
2. Central Business District
3. Industrial and Commercial Development
4. Human Relations and Welfare
5. Parks, Recreation, and Open Space
6. Cultural and Historical Resources and Development
7. Education and Libraries
8. Health and Sanitation (including water and sewage)
9. Highways, Public Transportation, Parking, and Traffic
10. Housing Resources
11 Public Safety

12. Technical Advisory Committee
13. Public Education

This list suggests the range of issues and problems which ought to be brought into a central perspective. Where the work of one committee is very closely related to that of another, there should be some dual membership. For example, recreation is related not only to parks, but also to education and probably to human relations (especially if juvenile delinquency is considered part of that committee's charge).

Either the main technical people working in the particular substantive areas, should be accorded committee membership or they should be separately constituted as a panel of consultants. One of the main advantages of these devices is that they bring together technical experts and program administrators operating in the same general area. It is also important that they be assembled in the presence of citizen representation. Such representation helps discipline the empire-building impulse and places a premium on statesmanship. It mitigates one of the greatest obstacles to progress in most communities, the lack of communication between various program personnel operating in the same general area of responsibility. A further advantage of this approach is that it expedites the education of the citizen members. *Ad hoc* committees have often been useless because the citizens seldom had time to grasp the intricacies of the subject in hand. They, therefore, tend either to be intimidated by the experts or to act ignorantly. Such continuing committees should create a citizen cadre of high competence.

The technical advisory committee, comprised of technical experts representing the various subject areas, serves a particularly important purpose. It includes both public and private individuals of technical competence. If the area has a college or university its personnel could be employed to advantage at this point. The committee should also include the top technical staff of the metropolitan citizens' council. Its basic objective would be to examine the adequacy of existing data for effective planning on a metropolitan basis. It should study the institutional processes by which information and facts are produced in order to facilitate the collection, integration, and distribution of data for rational decision-making. It would discover gaps in data and make proposals for filling them. It would investigate duplicated effort and make recommendations for the more efficient utilization of technical competence.

One approach toward improving planning in the metropolitan area is to create as much uniformity as possible in the assembly and distribution of relevant data. Every particular plan of consequence has an effect upon the total course of community development. Since it is desirable that as far as possible these plans be made against the background of all the relevant information, it is first necessary to identify this data. Some of it is in city departments, some in the county, a part in the towns or suburbs, much in state departments and special districts, and a good deal in federal agencies. In addition, much important data is collected by private business organizations, and semi-public organizations such as the Council of Social Agencies. Unfortunately, many of the facts that should be available are not, because the records of the private or public organizations involved have not been kept with a view toward serving the total planning needs of the community. With a little extra effort the data-gathering and record-keeping system of one organization could often be made useful to other agencies. As suggested in the previous chapter, much of this work of coordination could be undertaken by a state agency (for example, an Office of Local Affairs) if such existed. However, until the state undertakes this function it could be a prime responsibility of the technical advisory committee.

The planning of data collection and distribution is one of the most effective moves toward achieving more rational decisions in the metropolitan community. Clearly it does not solve the basic conflicts of interest, but it can eliminate much of the conflict due to ignorance. An approach which encourages policy-makers, either public or private, to view their decisions in relation to other plans also provides a basis for public discussion and consideration which can nurture the formulation of issues on a broader scale. At present, discussion is often parochial because our system encourages narrow formulation. The technical advisory committee could help provide more intelligent bases for discussion.

In the initial stages of development a citizens' council may be concerned primarily with establishing the planning and research base for effective action in the metropolitan area. However, in the long run it must be an action organization in the sense that it tries to develop community consensus and actively agitates for its program. This bridge to action is made much easier if the existing political leadership is woven into the organization. It is also desirable to involve the potential political leadership, since it is obviously unwise to encourage opposition. Politicians out of power are on the prowl for issues. The guiding principle is that whoever has the capacity to create trouble should be included if at all possible. Let the politicians compete with each other in advancing schemes and ideas to promote the common welfare. Above all, one should attempt partially to detach a politician from his parochial constituency and to fasten his future to a broader perspective.

We come back to the necessity of public education as one of the main functions of such a council. We must find ways of binding more citizens, as well as politicians, to the interests of the whole region. This probably means that one of the first research projects which should be conducted is an assesesment of the ideas and attitudes of various classes and groups of citizens. This will help the council to program its work. The first issues to be pushed will be those about which there is already some public understanding. Such a study will also indicate the main areas requiring attention in a program of public education. Moreover, it will suggest the nature of the citizen's attachment to the local community and the nature of his fear of larger governmental units. This understanding is necessary in order to develop programs which do the least amount of damage to the love of home rule and other local values. Such a study would also indicate the extent to which lack of information is an impediment. Differentiation should be made between the citizens generally and their opinion leaders, and different approaches should be developed for the dissemination of the necessary information.

There need to be special educational programs for various issues and categories of people. A good part of the educational process is involvement in committee work. However, once interest or concern is aroused a more systematic approach should be developed for those with sufficient time and interest. This requires an adult education program in the various substantive areas as well as in the elements of effective planning. It means study of the broad political, social, and economic forces which are at work. Material of both a general and a local nature should be distributed where it will do the most good. The mass media also have a prominent role to play. They may need a new kind of expertness to play the role effectively. In addition, we should use existing organizations for the transmission of facts and the discussion of plans. We should also be concerned about the quality of our social studies work in the public and private schools. They have a responsibilty to train our students in effective citizen participation.

Perhaps the most critical element in the creation of a metropolitan citizens' council is its composition. We have already commented on the importance of its relation to the governmental structure. In addition, three principles are crucial. First, as has been demonstrated over and over again, it is essential to get the support of the main commercial and industrial interests of the community. The effective organizations have succeeded in doing this. Some groups, dedicated to restricted programs, have confined themselves to this kind of representation. In recent years businessmen have come alive in community after community. Their natural disposition makes them capable of developing an enormous drive for action. They are also important because of their economic power. Their support is necessary to implement many plans. For example, downtown cannot be revived without the most dedicated kind of support from the business community. Planning that ignores the needs of industrial expansion is almost certain to fail. In addition, the financial support of an effective council will normally come in substantial measure from the business community. The economic stake of businessmen in the community justifies substantial expenditures on their part. However, complete dependence on this source should be avoided. You cannot get along without them but you dare not depend exclusively upon them.

Second, the "idea" people must be part of the council. Businessmen still too often assume that economic power automatically establishes the validity of their ideas about the future of the community. Nothing could be less true. In many communities businessmen have demonstrated that they do not even perceive what their own interests require, let alone what the public interest is. The "idea" men may come from anywhere. They may be merchants, industrialists, or bankers. They may be professional men or public administrators. Often they are university people, staff members of social agencies, or religious leaders. They may come from several steps down in a hierarchy as well as from the top. In our culture we foolishly assume that an exalted post entitles the individual to speak on everything. Therefore, if the university is to be represented, the usual selection is the president or a vice-president. We forget that the president was selected for his educational or fundraising ability and assume that his ideas on community development are entitled to more weight than those of a mere professor who has devoted much thought to the matter. The presence of the president may be important, but usually more for the symbol of commitment on the part of the institution than for his contribution of ideas. If he is also good at this so much the better; the point to bear in mind is that institutional leadership and ideas about the community's future are not necessarily synonymous. We need both.

Producing ideas is not achieved by hiring technical experts, although that too is necessary. Experts are hired for a purpose; the statement of that purpose conditions their work. If the council asks the wrong questions it is difficult to get meaningful answers. Often the technical staff can do much to educate the citizen leadership, but this is much more readily achieved if at least part of the leadership already has some sophistication or understanding. The possibility of the professional staffs educating the citizen leadership is further restricted by the process of hiring. Usually the preferred professionals will be those who show a disposition to see the matter in substantially the same terms as the employers.

Third, the council must be representative. You cannot afford to leave any powerful group out. Our politics at the local level is largely a politics of veto in which it is easier to prevent action disturbing to the *status quo* than it is to undertake bold new schemes. Any substantial group has a great capacity for protecting itself from proposals it considers harmful to its interests. On the other hand, even the most powerful group has difficulty promoting its new program if other groups are opposed. Our system of government and our attitudes toward government make it easier to prevent than to secure action. This condition in part results from the fact that on most matters large numbers of our citizens are apathetic and poorly informed. Consequently, if one group wants something new and another group opposes it the poorly informed and somewhat apathetic citizen is naturally disposed to maintain the *status quo*. The general feeling apparently is that it is better to prevent a wrong than to secure a new advantage. It is, therefore, desirable that any major proposals be for the general good and not merely for the advantage of a particular group. The formulation of such proposals requires discussion and consultation with all major elements in the community. A particular danger is that some men, if not consulted, will oppose a proposal not so much on its merits but simply because they were not consulted. This is a fact of human nature that must be kept in mind when the membership of a metropolitan citizens' council is being selected. Normally this means that the interests included must contain all the different business and industrial interests, labor, religious groups, professional groups, civic associations and minority interests, social agencies, and educational institutions.

Many businessmen have a natural repugnance toward this procedure. First of all, they are not accustomed to meeting with representatives of many of these groups and therefore feel uncomfortable. Also the perspective of many of these people will seem strange to business leaders; yet it is precisely the accommodation of these perspectives that is required for community consensus. One of the great advantages of the mixture is that it forces the discussion into a consideration of the good of the community with all factors involved. The good for any particular group is not an acceptable basis for discussion. This has a beneficial effect upon all concerned. Second, businessmen will often want action and insist upon getting down to work. Bringing in a lot of other people creates the danger of delay. However, too great an emphasis upon action may get short-term results but is apt to build up opposition over the long haul. The only secure basis for community development is full consideration of all the important concerns of the community.

The principle of representation is especially important if a metropolitan citizens' council is to serve its most creative function. One of the basic reasons for its existence is the inadequacy of the present governmental system. Some of the functions which such a council might perform could be taken over by government if proper political institutions existed. Therefore, the citizens' council should be viewed, in part, as a bridge to governmental reorganization. Such reorganization will need to be based upon the broadest possible consensus. It is one of the functions of the council to help establish that consensus. This in turn is possible only if all segments of the metropolitan community have confidence in the objectivity and public spirit of the council, a confidence best produced by systematic involvement of all important community interests. Informal government, no less than formal government, derives its legitimacy from the principle of representation. However, we have emphasized the representation of interests rather than organizations. Too much direct representation of organizations yields individuals who are not only concerned with the interests they represent but also have a vested interest in an organizational system that may be obsolete. We do not conclude that organizations should never be represented, but rather suggest control by the higher principle of interest representation.

The purpose of this model of citizen organization is not so much to suggest the form which such organization should take but rather to suggest the values to be sought. The basic need is for some framework in which one problem can be properly related to other problems. That is, we must create the context in which rational discussion can occur. Therefore, the metropolitan citizens' council is proposed as a method of overcoming obstacles to communication and providing a forum which can consider issues in their total context. Such a model council should also be considered as a bridge to political reorganization and to a more formal political forum. In practice individual communities will start where they are and often adapt existing institutions to this new need. The critical point is that there is now need for such an organization or its equivalent. This is especially true for those communities in which truly metropolitan government is still some distance away.

8

Mastery of the Metropolis

Our main purpose has been to suggest the variety and scope of the considerations involved in achieving mastery of the metropolis. However, we have not fully developed any of the considerations raised. Many will feel that we have not adequately discussed the administrative problems, state-local and interlocal relations, or other factors. It was not our purpose to do so. Many scholars are at work on particular aspects of the urban environment. The present effort has profited enormously from these studies. We have tried to suggest the variety of perspectives from which the urban problem should be viewed, to indicate the range of creative discretion available, to comment on the controlling political values, and make some suggestions for the strategy of progress.

PERSPECTIVES

We began our discussion by observing that planning for the future of our metropolitan areas was generally as fragmentary as our governmental structure and the free enterprise system. There have been some proposals for unified metropolitan government in recent years, but psychologically these proposals have usually been premature. Governmental reorganization is scarcely a dream to excite the imagination, especially since certain values inhere, or are reputed to inhere, in our dispersed governmental arrangements. Governmental reorganization will seldom be achieved by appeals to efficiency, partly because the evidence supporting the claim to greater efficiency is seldom very convincing, and partly because as a single value efficiency is often incapable of overriding the imputed virtues of local control. Reorganization is much more apt to occur when it seems essential to the creation of some facility or the adequate performance of some service which the community clearly desires. A community may even agree to annexation if its water supply or sewage disposal facilities, for instance, depend upon it. As important as this kind of lever is, it is scarcely adequate for creating a general governmental reorganization in our metropolitan areas.

We are caught in a kind of vicious circle. The fragmented economic and political structure gives rise to short-term and partial planning. The need for better planning and services leads to proposals for governmental reorganization. Such proposals are seldom popular because they do not seem essential to the solution of the service problems and because long-range planning is not a need felt strongly enough. Consequently, when the proposals are defeated we content ourselves with ameliorating problems as they arise. Our first premise was that governmental reorganization would provide a basis for more fundamental and imaginative planning, but we soon discovered that without substantive dreams and aspirations for the future of our urban environment it was usually difficult to improve governmental structure. The dreams depend on the structure and the structure on the dreams. This tendency of one factor to reinforce the other needs to be converted from a vicious circle into a hopeful pathway.

To achieve this result our approach has been two-fold. First, we should deliberately divorce ourselves from practical considerations in part of our efforts.[1] Some people, at least, should forget about the pragmatics and address themselves to the potentialities of the urban environment. Their task should be to create an image of the future, a substantive image concerned with the kind of life that is now technologically and economically possible.[2] We should talk

[1] An imaginative proposal for an elected Metropolitan Direction-Finding Commission to prepare a 25-year set of social-physical goals is Robert C. Hoover, "On Master Plans and Constitutions," *The Journal of the American Institute of Planners*, February, 1960, pp. 5 ff.

[2] An interesting series of articles dealing with the possibilities for metropolitan areas generally is in *The Future Metropolis*, Daedalus, Winter, 1961.

about what we want to be, how we want to live, how we want to work, play, and consume: what the actual content of a delightful urban existence should be for an enormous variety of people. Let us overleap all the difficulties for a moment and try to discover what we are missing. If we can construct a compelling image of the potentialities of our urban civilization then we can return to the question of how to achieve it. Unless some such image exists it is doubtful that sufficient motive force can be generated to transform our institutions.

The second approach is more practical and accepts the connection between structure and planning. If we cannot proceed directly to a governmental organization which will then encourage better planning and more imaginative ideas, perhaps we can create less formal organizations which will stimulate these ideas. It is at this point that the development of rather informal political organizations of legislative or executive personnel drawn from the whole metropolitan area can be very useful. Such organizations provide a context for raising more fundamental problems than do existing legal jurisdictions. Perhaps even more important are the citizen organizations which can deal with issues in terms of their total context. Such organizations, especially if they hire professional staff and include a close connection with the existing political leadership, are in a position both to create a substantive image of the greater city's future and to develop the public understanding and those expectations which are the condition of major progress. In our metropolitan areas, as in the underdeveloped countries, we need a "revolution of rising expectations."

Our concern for the quality of urban existence quickly leads us beyond the sphere of public action. Not only is private action necessary to stimulate the dream of a brighter urban future and pave the way to governmental reorganization, but the texture of urban life is finally determined as much by myriad private decisions as by governmental action, no matter how grandly conceived. This leads to several conclusions. One is that the private concentration of capital, and therefore private planning, is potentially one of the more hopeful elements in revitalizing our older cities and in raising our standards for the new communities yet to be built. One may hope that in the future we will build more towns and fewer subdivisions. Development on a large scale should lead to a higher standard of social amenity than results from the present patchwork. The same observation applies to the advantage which large urban renewal tracts have over small urban parcels. In both instances it becomes the responsibility of the developer to create the environment as well as the structures. Therefore, one hopes that, for example, Robert Dowling will succeed in the development of Sterling Forest without too many concessions to short-term economic returns. A few such successes could raise the human standard for our metropolitan expansion. Indeed, improved results will come not only from larger aggregations of capital but perhaps even more from viewing such developments in terms of their long-term economic potential rather than as a source of quick profits. The highest immediate return often results in a smaller long-term return.

Since the dominant pattern will probably remain one of a large number of individual property owners in our urban areas, the necessary private planning requires much more private co-operation than we have been accustomed to in the past. We already see this cooperation in many places in the effort to revitalize our downtown areas. The efforts range all the way from limited objectives, such as more parking, to a complete plan for the central business district. As the urban renewal program becomes more concerned with rehabilitation of existing areas, in addition to its early emphasis upon redevelopment, the need for neighborhood cooperation becomes apparent. The government can improve the framework of neighborhood services and facilities, but the quality of environment will still depend largely on individual homeowners and businessmen. Their efforts will be greatly stimulated by a public-private plan for revitalization. Individuals are discouraged from taking solitary action unless there is a reasonable expectation that the environment will be changed along with the individual structure.

The combination of public and private action is required primarily by our desire to achieve the maximum potential from an urban civilization. It was not so important when we were concerned only with achieving minimums and preventing the worst abuses. This objective could be achieved by governmental policy. The competition between cities (and between suburbs as well) is greatly stimulated by the accelerated obsolescence which characterizes our culture. In the past we have thought about this phenomenon in terms of the rapid rate of obsolescence for automobiles, home appliances, or drugs. However, the accelerated obsolescence of capital investment in industry, together with greater freedom from old locational considerations, has stimulated the competitive struggle between cities. No longer can a city rest secure on its existing economic base. It is sure to be obsolete in a few years and some of it need not be replaced in the same location.

Aesthetics and social amenities become a matter of survival. In deciding upon location industries are typically interested in the educational, cultural, recreational, and other facilities as well as the cheapness of the land, the tax rate, public utilities, and the available labor supply. They will probably become even more broadly concerned in the future. One can generalize by saying that communities which are attractive and pleasant places in which to live will have a competitive advantage. Cities are attractive and pleasant because of enlightened *public and private* policy.

THE RANGE OF DISCRETION

One difficulty with much of our thinking about the future is the necessity of using mental counters from our past experience. We can see the shape of an imagined golden past much more readily than we can see the shape of a substantially new paradise. Therefore, we tend to idealize the nineteenth- or early twentieth-century city and ask how we can recapture it. We are not really interested in recapturing the whole, but only some aspects of it that have been lost. Thus we may seek to reconstruct the transportation system in an earlier image because we dislike what the automobile has done. Or we may feel a decline in neighborliness and therefore desire a revival of the alleged virtues of the old neighborhood.

More particularly we may think of the suburb as the reincarnation of the legendary virtues of the nineteenth-century town. Little do we realize the enormous distance between the two.

For better or worse much of our life has been irrevocably nationalized and even internationalized. It is futile to resist these national and world forces. It is the part of wisdom to accommodate our lives and local communities to them. Nonetheless, it is necessary to mitigate some of the negative consequences which these forces often have for the local community. It also is necessary to find substitutes for some old institutions or values which have been destroyed.

We have indicated some of the national and world forces which limit the range of local discretion. Our discussion was suggestive rather than exhaustive. Certain consequences of modern technology are rather readily discernible in broad outline. The impact of the motor car has already been well chronicled. There is no reason to expect any fundamental reversal in our pattern of urban sprawl. At a number of critical points it can be modified. We can plan for greater dependence upon public transportation than we have been doing. We can take account of special groups, such as the aged, who may need public transportation. We can find devices for encouraging people to make more use of mass transit and less of the private car when going downtown. This is especially vital in our largest cities. Nonetheless, improved means of communication, better roads, cheaper power transmission, and other technological forces or devices will certainly result in a continued pattern of urban sprawl. Our best hope is to plan the growth better and to provide alternatives for those people who find the central cities attractive. Thus we can influence the rate at which the dispersion occurs and its character, but it is futile to try and recapture the city of the early twentieth century.

We need to find ways of making creative use of new technological advances rather than to beat our breasts about their consequences. Most such advances have been looked upon by some people as threats to civilization. We spend too much time, for example, clucking our tongues about the limitations of television and too little discussing how it could be a more positive cultural force. If we are going to address ourselves seriously to the potentialities of technology for the urban environment we need clarification of our goals and purposes. We need to construct imaginatively the alternative urban environments which are now technically feasible and culturally desirable. Our social policy should then be directed toward finding ways of experimenting with the possibilities. This is much more difficult than with industrial production, since it means the creation of new environments.

Beyond the experimentation we need to create imaginative environments which are not yet technically feasible in order to direct our research. Again this is easier to do in industry, since the goal of a plane manufacturer is to get a plane that is faster, safer, more efficient, or will carry a greater load than existing planes. The new goals are merely extensions of existing goals. In urban development it is easier to discover the new aims for parts of the environment than for the environment as a whole. Thus we can identify rather readily certain goals for the housing industry, but for the neighborhood they are not so easily discerned. However, goals for the urban environment and a variety of conceptions as to the content of the good life are necessary in order to identify the technical progress which is required.

The nationalization of industry, finance, and commerce alters the capacity of local areas to meet their problems. Many decisions which affect the local area are made by company headquarters in New York or some other large city. The local managers primarily implement company policy. Therefore, the local community operates within a context of centralized economic power. This does not mean that the local community is powerless to influence these decisions, but it does mean that they are made in terms of the self-interest of national corporations. This is another element in the heightened competitive struggle between cities. Just as local officials find that more and more of their time is devoted to negotiating with state and federal officials, so also those who are interested in improving a local community's economic base must acquire an understanding of the workings of the national economic hierarchies. Close study must be made of the changing locational factors important in determining national corporate policies. Those communities will prosper most which make an effort to understand the constantly changing requirements of industry and commerce. While such considerations limit local discretion in a sense, they also provide an opportunity. The accelerated rate of change which characterizes our economy provides a special opportunity for remaking our urban environment according to our heart's desires. With good planning and foresight a community may have several choices concerning the pattern of its development. The very flux and mobility of our system provides an opportunity for reshaping the economic base of many communities. A community does not have to settle for unguided industrial expansion but may be able to encourage what seems to it the most desirable kind.

The nationalization of our economic life has a particularly powerful impact upon the supply of local leadership. It is especially encouraging that many national corporations are urging their managerial personnel to take an active part in community affairs. Labor unions for some time have encouraged local political participation but have been somewhat slow to push activity of a more general nature. Because of the mobility of the managerial class at least two elements are needed for vital local leadership. First, the relatively short-term managers must be readily accepted into existing organizations. They cannot be expected to serve a long apprenticeship before being acknowledged as "community leaders." In too many communities the old families try to hold too tight a rein. Second, the basis of permanent participation must be expanded. In most communities there is an untapped potential leadership with a permanent residence. One thinks of the doctors who generally have a poor record of performance considering their status and income. Many other professional groups, including architects, teachers, and engineers, could also do a good deal more. In many communities this means acknowledging that business plus the legal profession is too narrow a leadership base, particularly when so many of the leading businessmen are short-term residents.

The changes in the amount of leisure and in the age distribution of our population create great new opportunities for local communities. We must recognize these changes, accept them, and then inquire into their implications. The increase in leisure and in the number of retired people means that greater variety and more choice in environments and consumer patterns are being demanded. Communities which plan for this richness of possibilities will greatly increase their attractiveness. The multiplication of products in industry has its corollary in the variety of patterns of urban living.

The question of minority groups probably troubles our urban areas more than any other social issue. It has been our contention that we are approaching a period of stability as far as the numbers of colored people are concerned, as we have already reached a comparable stability of our Puerto Rican population. The main trend of the years ahead will be the gradual dispersal of our colored population throughout the metropolitan area. The period of ghetto building among Negroes has probably reached its climax. The international situation, our own ideology, the economic and educational progress of the Negro—all conspire to achieve residential as well as educational integration. Successful communities will find ways of achieving this integration smoothly. Communities which are less successful in handling the process of residential integration will suffer competitively. On the other hand, there is little reason for expecting any substantial abandonment of our policy of socio-economic segregation in neighborhoods. It is likely that in metropolitan areas with large Negro populations we will have a pattern of dispersed segregated areas voluntarily chosen by Negroes or other minority groups as well as an over-all integrated pattern. This results from the fact that much of the demand for integration is really a demand for equal access to housing and a higher standard of social amenity.

In general, we can say that those communities will fare best who recognize and accept the context of national forces within which they must operate. Nothing is so futile as acting as though one has a kind of choice which does not in fact exist. However, once we have acknowledged the limits of our choice, technology and affluence open up an enormous range of possibilities. We must simply have the wit to grasp them.

POLITICAL VALUES

The most fundamental political and social value to be sought in planning the future of our cities and towns is the need for maximum freedom of choice for our citizens. We have already noted that this requires the elimination of artificial restraints upon the capacity of minority groups to choose. In the long run the more fundamental problem is to increase the range of choices available. Our people are infinitely diverse. They desire an endless variety of choices in homes, neighborhoods, and cities. Each urban area should attempt to provide as many different types of environment as the market will support. Cities should also attempt to develop their own particular flavor. Mass communication and industrial standardization need not standardize cities and suburbs. Certainly many of the parts will be standard, but the way the parts are put together and the way people use the city admits of more local experimentation than we have had the nerve to undertake.

There is no ideal city, no single design which is universally best. We cannot afford to get a fixed image of what a neighborhood, town, or city ought to be. In home construction we have been too obsessed with the single detached house on a suburban lot. Government policy and the policies of lending institutions have discouraged experimentation. Our architects, or perhaps their more cautious clients, have preferred standard solutions to the housing problem. We need more experimentation in housing and especially in the total residential environment in order to satisfy the differences in the condition and taste of our citizens. Our objective should be to provide the same range of choices in styles of life as mass production has made possible in styles of clothes. As in the apparel industry there should be a wide range of choice for the poor as well as for the wealthy.

This variety and choice can be achieved only by large-scale planning. We need to be able to plan for the total metropolitan area, not so much to provide adequate services or efficiency, as to realize the full potential of the environment for the variety of alternatives which a diverse population requires. The criticism of partial, half-hearted planning is that it cannot encompass the range of choices which our technology and wealth make theoretically possible.

We need to initiate more imaginative consumer research for our cities. We need to discover what existing needs are unmet. We already know that certain kinds of housing are not being adequately supplied. We can discover the discontents and dissatisfactions which now exist so that we can plan the future more nearly in terms of human needs. The more difficult problem is the translation of discontent into a positive image. We must develop better techniques for discovering what would be pleasing to various categories of urban residents, since men know better what they dislike than what they like. It may sound somewhat crass to suggest applying the techniques of gauging the market for new car design to the problems of city planning, but we are already using them in some areas. The New York Public Library uses good market techniques in locating branch libraries. This is the only sensible way to do it.

In the final analysis it is not a question of what the world-famous planner thinks downtown should be, it is rather a question of what our population will patronize or can be led to patronize. The canons of beauty, comfort, convenience, and excitement for urban reconstruction are not subject to abstract determination, but are finally determined by the habits and reactions of the public or segments of it. We should remind ourselves that there is seldom one public but rather there are many publics. We cannot permit one to deny the legitimate aims of another. Therefore, the genius of planning is not to employ a planner with magnificent schemes in his mind but rather to employ one who can discover the deepest desires and needs of multiple publics and translate those needs into attractive plans and programs. We should not allow the egomania of the planner to be imposed on the city, but rather the planner should give form and design to the needs and aspirations of a varied public.

In a democratic society effective planning and public education are different aspects of the same thing. It is wholly desirable to create imaginative, even magnificent, plans for the metropolis. However, we should not forget that one of the great benefits of such plans is that they give a well developed context for carrying on public discussion of goals and purposes. Therefore, such a plan should never be *sold* to the public direct from the planning office. The planner should not feel the need of defending its every feature. A good preliminary plan is one step in the process of conducting a public discussion of the future of the metropolis and its people; it is one which raises the fundamental questions which need clarification, resolution, or compromise. Planners cannot fully anticipate how all the forces will work out.

The emphasis probably should be upon alternatives rather than the construction of *a plan*. We need to ask the city to discuss the choices which confront it. Therefore, the planner, as well as the political and civic leadership generally, have a first responsibility to construct the public debate in meaningful terms. When all the interests are consulted, when all the values have been held up to scrutiny, and when alternative syntheses have been explored, intelligent public decision can be taken.

One of the main advantages of creating a comprehensive citizens' organization is that it provides the basis for imaginative formulation and discussion of the issues confronting the local community. By encouraging citizen participation we can bring more of the relevant considerations to bear upon policy formation. A continuing conversation between private groups and between these groups and public officials is the condition both of intelligent policy formation and of the public understanding necessary for secure progress.

Public education is also promoted by other devices. For example, knowledge of what is going on in other cities, even other countries, is very important. Nothing stimulates a citizen more than an example of a creative project which he has viewed in operation. The activity of our local business leaders in recent years has been stimulated by the example of other cities which they have viewed in their travels.

We cannot afford in our programs of public education to over-simplify the problems and issues. To do so is to court disillusion-ment. Comprehensive citizen organization greatly aids putting the problem in its proper context. To implement this, an educational program for civic and governmental leaders is needed. Such a program must create some degree of sophistication about the com-plexity of the social fabric. Too many of our programs for com-munity leaders are oriented toward group dynamics. Most communities have a great many residents skilled in group re-lations, but few have any significant number who can grasp the substance of issues and relate one cluster to another.

The basic political principle arising from all this complexity is the need to create patterns of authority which correspond more closely to the dimensions of our problems. In the long run this means a reorganization of our political system, but the pre-condi-tion of that reorganization is greater public awareness of the complexity of "local" issues. As we have seen, many local activities are subject to state or national determination of certain minimum standards. These standards have the important by-product of tempering the competition between localities. Much state and na-tional effort is directed at encouraging high standards of local service or a more congenial local environment.

State and national grants-in-aid to localities should not be used to destroy local discretion. However, such grants should be condi-tioned so that they stimulate redefinitions of what is "local." For example, state aid to education has forced the centralization of small school districts. Because of local jealousies and conflicts such centralization proceeds slowly if left entirely to voluntary local action. One of the basic functions of state aid to education has been to force a reformulation of the meaning of "local" so that it corresponds more nearly to contemporary educational needs. Therefore, central government must be concerned with more than encouraging existing local units to undertake activities and provide services which are now deemed essential. Aid must be provided in such a way that the central support goes to jurisdictions which make sense in terms of the scope of the problem. In some cases this means the creation of new units of local government which supersede old and smaller units of local government. State and national activity on the local scene can often be used to strengthen local government if central power is used to force or encourage the destruction of some local loyalties by creating others more in harmony with present reality.

STRATEGY OF PROGRESS

The basic proposition of urban development which includes all other aspects is the desirability of creating a base which will facilitate political and social adaptation. The preceding discussion includes many elements of a strategy of progress for our urban areas. Especially important is the creation of a metropolitan citizens' council or its equivalent. The emphasis upon public education is also part of any general strategy. Citizen participation and public education are vitally important because they are necessary to sustain progress. In themselves they solve nothing, but they are the condition of progress. However, in addition to the elements already discussed there are several other matters of great importance.

A subsidiary general proposition is the desirability of creating those permanent or temporary informal arrangements among public officials which improve communication, stimulate discussion of common problems, and provide a sounding board for broad proposals. Such arrangements include organizations of elected officials, chief executives, the executives in functional areas, and technicians. In the two latter regions state and federal officials may sometimes be included. It is interesting that our civilization, which has enormously expedited the processes of communication, finds lack of communication one of its great difficulties. In most metropolitan areas the level of communication is very low between public employees who have common problems. Therefore, the creation of the Inter-County Supervisors Committee in the Detroit metropolitan area and the New York Metropolitan Council are hopeful signs for improved communication between public officials in metropolitan areas.

Within a given city also, communication may be inadequate.

A city as large and complex as New York has particular difficulty making sure that the left hand knows what the right hand is doing. Within the city improved communication may often be secured by structural changes which achieve communication by centralizing authority or making the mayor more effective. The staff services of a central personnel or budgeting agency are justified more by their tendency to increase the capacity of the mayor to coordinate the parts than by the criteria of efficiency or program effectiveness. The examples of New Haven and Philadelphia are particularly instructive. They suggest that the modern mayor needs two different kinds of coordinating expertness at his disposal. He needs an expert to manage and coordinate the old-line city departments. In New Haven this function is performed by the Director of Administration; in Philadelphia, by the Chief Administrative Officer. However, the problems with which we have been dealing also require the coordination of just those elements which are most critical in determining the future of the city. In New Haven this function is performed by the Development Administrator who has responsibility for planning, urban renewal, code enforcement, and traffic and parking; in Philadelphia, by the Development Co-ordinator. Mayor Lee of New Haven calls his Development Administrator the "Deputy Mayor for the Future." Few mayors are technically qualified to provide the technical leadership for either the operational or developmental side of city administration. Therefore, part of the strategy of progress is to provide him with these tools.

However, the creation of the office of Development Administrator does not solve all the problems of communication. Usually the schools and the housing agency have some degree of autonomy. In addition many of the operating departments, particularly their capital improvements programs, need to be integrated into an urban renewal program. Therefore, the need for discussion, clearance, and education remains vital. Indeed, any large organization is now so complex that the problems of coordination and policy formation cannot be totally accommodated by the organization chart, but must be supplemented with more or less elaborate devices to keep the necessary information flowing to the right places at the right time. The main need for city administration is to provide the chief executive officer with suitable technical assistance.

We have already commented in this summary on the strategy of using state and national grants-in-aid to encourage the reclustering of local political authority. The state has an important role to play because of its sovereign position. The state needs to provide the legal and constitutional means for local experimentation and adaptation. Local action must be permitted to transform the county into a general purpose government, especially when the development of urban counties constitute an answer, or partial answer, to the metropolitan problem. This is not a panacea, since the county is hopelessly inadequate in New England, and since in many metropolitan areas the problems transcend county lines. However, in many of these the county is still a more comprehensive unit than the city. Even a relatively small city may be located on the edge of the county and consequently have its metropolitan area in more than one county. The creation of urban counties cannot be a general answer to our metropolitan problems. Still, since this device seems to hold more promise than any other particular approach at the moment, it should be encouraged. As a matter of strategy it may be desirable to concentrate on the reorganization of the county before attempting to convert it into a government of general jurisdiction. Especially urgent is the provision of countywide political and administrative leadership. If this requirement can be sufficiently met then we can think seriously of transferring urban functions to this old rural entity.

The state also needs to remove the legal obstacles to interlocal cooperative arrangements. Local jurisdictions should be encouraged to take common action when the subject requires it. In this area state administrative agencies can play a stimulating and sometimes coercive role. We have used the example of education; but public health, social services, pollution control, hospitals, water supply, and many other areas are of both state and local concern. The state has a responsibility to provide the legal means for interlocal cooperation as well as to use the legal power vested in its own administrative agencies to encourage that cooperation. The state should not become obsessed with the abstraction called "home rule" and indiscriminately shore up towns and villages by helping them to perform services or provide facilities which ought better to be provided on a broader basis. The state should be solicitous about home rule, but interpret that piety to mean local control on a basis commensurate with the dimensions of the problem. Shoring up existing local units may mean rendering the metropolitan community incapable of effective action, as is illustrated by the encouragement of full-scale town or village planning. It is more important that the planning of such small units be restricted in scope and the planning of the "local" county be expanded.

The final and most self-evident element in a strategy of progress is the development of civic and political leadership. On the civic level it means insisting that the most able people devote time and energy to the local community. It means an open-door policy of inviting new and younger people into positions of responsibility. It means encouraging the institutions in which people earn their living to develop a policy of stimulating participation in local affairs. Effective local leadership will develop fastest if it is brought into close relationship with professional staff.

Probably no other single element is more important than competent political leadership, and no aspect of political leadership is more important than the quality of the central city mayor or city manager. He is in the best position to exercise areawide leadership. He normally has more political power than any other individual in the area. If we reconstructed our counties and elected a county executive on a countywide basis, this official would gradually become the most important political figure. In the meantime the mayor fills that position. All over the country there is new interest in his office. There is new understanding of the skills which the office requires. The modern mayor must lead the total community and not just administer a standard set of departments. He must reach out beyond the city boundaries and beyond the traditional field of public activity into the private area. Here he cannot command, but he can lead. The mayor should be an educator, conciliator, initiator, and stimulator even more than an administrator. He is the focal point of public attention in the difficult process of shaping and reshaping our urban environment.

EPILOGUE

At the end let us go back to the beginning. The purpose of all this interest and activity is, first, to discover what we expect of life in our new urban culture and second, to see how we can fulfill such a promise.

City planning in the United States was first seized by the "City Beautiful" movement. This was a good, though limited, dream. In the "City Practical" which succeeded it we gained something and lost something. Then came the "City of Welfare", which added a concern for our less fortunate citizens. We need now to recapture some of the spirit of the beautiful while keeping our feet firmly on the ground and maintaining our concern for minimum standards of human decency. However, we need more than beauty, practicality, and welfare: we need concern for the full range of urban values which can make the metropolis an exciting, vital, and pleasing human experience. We need now the "City of Expanding Amenities." Comprehensive planning must include both a broad geographic area and a broad spectrum of human values. Mastery of the metropolis cannot be gained with less.